T0309261

"Trust is the most important asset for any professional. In a world where some cut corners and try to game the system, this is a book about how to win by playing the long game and doing it right. You'll emerge a better marketer and a better leader."

Dorie Clark, author of *Reinventing You* and executive education faculty, Duke University Fuqua School of Business

Answers for Ethical Marketers

With recent changes in technology, media, and the communication landscape, the journey to ethics has become more complicated than ever before. This book aims to answer ethical questions, from applying ethics and sound judgment through your organization and communication channels to taking your ethics and values into every media interview. With the understanding of how personal and professional ethics align, business leaders, managers, and students will maneuver their way around this new landscape showcasing their values in ethical conduct.

This book is divided into eight important areas based on where and why a breakdown in ethical behavior is likely to occur, and delivers advice from experts on the frontlines of business communications who know what it means to face the inherent changes and challenges in this field. With more than 80 questions and answers focused on guiding marketing, PR and business professionals, readers will uncover situations where ethics are challenged, and their values will be tested.

This straightforward Q&A guidebook is for professionals who realize ethics are a crucial part of decision-making in their communications and who want to maintain trust with the public and their positive brand reputations in business. Readers will receive answers to pressing ethical questions to help them apply best practice guidelines and good judgment in their own situations, based on the stories, theories, and practical instruction from the author's 30 years of experience as well as the thought leaders featured in this book.

Deirdre K. Breakenridge is an author, entrepreneur and CEO at Pure Performance Communications. As a 30-year veteran in PR, marketing, and branding, she has worked with senior leaders at Fortune 500 companies.

Answers for Ethical Marketers

A Guide to Good Practice in Business Communication

Deirdre K. Breakenridge

Routledge
Taylor & Francis Group

NEW YORK AND LONDON

First published 2021
by Routledge
52 Vanderbilt Avenue, New York, NY 10017

and by Routledge
2 Park Square, Milton Park, Abingdon, Oxon OX14 4RN

Routledge is an imprint of the Taylor & Francis Group, an informa business

Library of Congress Cataloging-in-Publication Data
Names: Breakenridge, Deirdre, author.
Title: Answers for ethical marketers : a guide to good practice in business
  communication / Deirdre K. Breakenridge.
Description: New York : Routledge, 2021. | Includes bibliographical
  references and index.
Identifiers: LCCN 2020049370 (print) | LCCN 2020049371 (ebook) | ISBN
  9780367531072 (hardback) | ISBN 9780367529505 (paperback) | ISBN
  9781003080466 (ebook)
Subjects: LCSH: Marketing—Moral and ethical aspects. | Business
  communication. | Business ethics.
Classification: LCC HF5415 .B63634 2021 (print) | LCC HF5415
  (ebook) | DDC 174/.4–dc23
LC record available at https://lccn.loc.gov/2020049370
LC ebook record available at https://lccn.loc.gov/2020049371

ISBN: 9780367531072 (hbk)
ISBN: 9780367529505 (pbk)
ISBN: 9781003080466 (ebk)

Typeset in Sabon
by Taylor & Francis Books

To my loving husband Mark, thank you for going the distance, for helping to make dreams happen and for navigating the mountains along the way.

To my Mom and Dad, I'm forever grateful for your love and guidance.

To my children Megan, Matt, Nicole and our angel Noelle, whether you're biological or you came to me through family bond, I love you with all of my heart.

Thank you all for being with me on this life-long learning journey. XO

Contents

Acknowledgements   x
Author Biography   xiii
Foreword   xiv

Introduction: The Journey to Ethics: A Personal Choice &
Professional Practice   1

1   Learning the Essentials & the Overarching Ethical Lessons   7

2   Applying Ethics Through All Your Media Channels   26

3   Using Your Ethics in Cause Marketing   58

4   Taking Ethics to Media Interviews and Appearances   77

5   Filtering Ethics Through Your Organization   94

6   Learning Ethics from a Mentor   111

7   Being a Leader Means Being an Ethical Role Model   133

8   Embracing the Ethical Lessons   151

Index   156

Acknowledgements

Every book is a different experience and each one is a labor of love. I could not have written Answers for Ethical Marketers without the guidance, patience, support, and encouragement of hundreds of people in my network ... far too many to name in the Acknowledgements section of my book.

However, there are family members, colleagues, mentors, and business partners who have individually, and as a group, helped me on the journey. They've been instrumental in defining and redefining my ethics and values, as I have shared these beliefs through my communications and conduct for over 50 years. Through their insights and guidance, I can now share with you what I've learned in a Q&A guidebook.

Starting with my family ... you have shaped me into the person I am today, and you have helped me to grow. My mom and dad are the role models of a lifetime, showing me love, strength, kindness, incredible generosity and instilling this "ethics GPS" in me as I transitioned from childhood to adulthood and into my career. Of course, my brothers, Bill and Jay, were there alongside, often challenging me, as siblings growing up tend to do. They have made me "tougher" yet compassionate and ready to face the world. Now, with their extended families, my Sisters-in-Law, Sue and Tatiana, and all of my amazing nieces and nephews the strength, love and kindness know no bounds.

There is my beautiful daughter, Megan, who has been the light of my life for 25 years of my journey. The ethics and values I hold dear are intertwined in her, as if we are one. Together we have found the beauty in the simple, we have loved fully with our hearts and we have weathered storms together, all with a compass of love, truth, kindness, compassion and strength. I also want to give a warm shout out to two important people who have also helped in the shaping of Megan's journey. Jeff and Dylan, thank you.

The Skrobola Family (the entire clan) came into our lives unexpectedly. Quickly, we discovered a new excitement, love, zest for life and how to get over any obstacle as a family, and, at times, they were the largest mountains I had ever encountered. I could not have written this book without the strength of my other and sometimes better half. My loving husband, Mark, rarely gives himself credit for all the good in our lives. So, I will do that here, in my Acknowledgements section. Then, there are the step kids who are not step kids at all. They are my kids! Matt, Nicole and our dearest angel, Noelle, you, too, have shaped me into a better person and parent. Of course, the important people you have brought into my life, Casandra, Pavlos and Brian in Spain, you are also very much a part of the ethics and values journey.

On the business front, I'm grateful to collaborate with a team of professionals who are so much more than just business partners. Corina Manea, you have been one of the brightest, most loving and giving hearts in my life. Thank you for all that you do and how you continue to inspire me and the people around you. I know Mihai is also a big part of this "picture" and he is very much a strength and support system that I so greatly appreciate.

To other very special members of my team, Raquel Romero, Claire Donaldson (who was with us for a while and really left her mark), the ever-creative Gianna (my niece, Gigi), my journey would not have been the same nor could I have accomplished as much as I do every day in my creative endeavors and communications without you. Together, you have helped me to capture who I am and communicate all my ethics and values with passion and with a FEEL First approach.

Of course, I want to give a personal note of thanks to each and every Ethical Marketer who took the time to contribute to this book. First is friend and colleague Richard Bistrong, who wrote the book's Foreword. Richard has been on an amazing journey himself and I'm grateful to be a part of it. We met years ago, when Richard was finding his path and really showcasing his values and what it means to have ethical conduct in all your interactions. Richard's trajectory has focused on education and helping other professionals, based on some very intense experiences and learning lessons that are in his rear-view mirror.

Now, for the long list of friends, colleagues and professionals who have given a piece of themselves for this book in the spirit of mentoring others and creating a world and a media landscape that is better, kinder, more effective in the spirit of "doing the right thing" and with a "Do No Harm" attitude. A big thank you goes to Rebekah Iliff, Corina Manea, Wendy Glavin, Gini Dietrich, Martin Waxman, Dick Martin, Holly Golcher, Mark W. McClennan, Shonali Burke, Winnie Sun, Suzanne Brown, Stephanie Dalfonzo, Tess Kossow, Susan Freeman, Jason Mollica, Anthony D'Angelo, Ken Jacobs, Karen Freberg, Sheila Murphy, Michael Meath and Kate Isler.

This book would not have come together so smoothly if it wasn't for Routledge who believed in its potential. Thank you, Routledge publishing team, for helping me with both of my Answers books. Meredith Norwich has been a wonderful senior editor offering her guidance and along with her marketing team has taken a greater interest in my work, which no other publisher has done after 20 years of publishing books. Thank you for being supportive of your authors in a way that stands out from other publishing operations.

Now, for a thank you that goes out to each and every reader. You have been an inspiration for this book as I read your emails, tweets, Facebook and Instagram posts, and watch videos from YouTube, TikTok and Zoom. You are the reason why I wanted to answer questions about ethics and values in communications and to carve a path showcasing what it means to be an Ethical Marketer. I look forward to conversations on social media and ways to learn how you are doing and feeling about your communications, before, during and after you read this book. Although I'm answering questions and so are many other professionals in the pages of my book, please know that you, too, have guided me and I've learned from you in ways that you probably don't know.

Finally, thank you all for being a part of this journey and a roadmap to becoming an Ethical Marketer. Regardless of your profession, role or responsibilities, we are all in this together.

Author Biography

Deirdre K. Breakenridge is an author, entrepreneur and CEO at Pure Performance Communications. As a 30-year veteran in PR, marketing, and branding, she has worked with senior leaders at Fortune 500 companies.

Deirdre is a career-long storyteller and strategist, helping brands and professionals to ignite the energy of their communication, lead pressing media conversations and grow influence in the market. She's been working with leaders for decades to create award-winning PR and marketing programs and building relationships based on loyalty and advocacy.

Deirdre is the author of seven business books sharing stories and advice to navigate changing consumer behavior and an evolving media landscape. Her book, *Answers for Modern Communicators*, was published by Routledge and was recently named by Book Authority among the 100 Best Storytelling Books of All Time.

Deirdre has previously taught PR and social media courses, online and in the classroom for NYU, UMASS at Amherst, Rutgers University and Fairleigh Dickinson University. She took her passion for teaching to LinkedIn Learning and has also developed eight video courses on PR and marketing. Deirdre also speaks internationally on the topics of PR, marketing, branding, and social media communications.

Deirdre has been blogging at PR Strategies for over 10 years and she is also the host of the podcast, Women Worldwide, which in its fifth year has nearly 2 million downloads.

Foreword

I first became familiar with Deirdre Breakenridge's work when I read her book, co-authored with Brian Solis, *Putting the Public Back in Public Relations*. I read the book in 2012, and unpacking my notes, highlights and post-it book-marks to think about the foreword to *Answers for Ethical Marketers*, I think I got 'hooked' on *Putting the Public Back in Public Relations* book early on (page 39), where Deirdre shared how "brands today must show their human side by participating directly with the people they want to reach in the networks where they're active." And by the time I read her parting words that "in the social economy, relationships are the new currency," I realized I had just finished a 'game changing' work in my personal and professional life. Why? Because I was reading *Putting the Public Back in Public Relations* from the confines of a Federal Prison, where I was serving a fourteen and a half month prison sentence for violating the FCPA (the US anti-bribery law) and was contemplating what life might look like anew, *not* being an international sales Vice President.

So, one of the first calls I made when I was released from prison in December, 2013 was to Deirdre, asking if she could help me to think about how I could use my experience as an international sales executive who paid the ultimate price for corruption, the loss of liberty, and to see where sharing that journey might lead. Since then, the crucible of my conduct has transformed into a journey of moving from corruption to compliance as an ethics, compliance and anti-bribery consultant, and hence, the honor of writing this foreword for *Answers for Ethical Marketers*.

But who and what is an ethical marketer? Having worked with global organizations, including leadership, commercial and compliance teams, I think it's easily answered, even if not easily executed: All of us. In today's world of hyper-transparency, everything we do, what we say, how we say it, and where we say it, will be interpreted by different groups and cultures, and sometimes in different ways. Yet, in how ethics and ethical decisions should drive all our conduct, as Deirdre shares, "mistakes and mishaps will happen." And there's nothing wrong with that. As we grow our careers as communication professionals, and step into new roles, with rapid technological advances, even with the best of intentions "errors or missteps in communication" are going to occur. However, as I learned in my own work, if we are transparent when we end up on the 'sharp end' of an ethical dilemma, by sharing what happened and why it happened, we can use those mistakes, as regrettable as they might be, to improve processes and communications across the organization. To me, that's an ethical marketer. When you have the courage to share and learn from your mistakes and errors, you are putting power in your voice, by transparency and honesty.

As communication professionals, you are the gatekeepers to your company's values, culture, and ethics. While tone at the top, inspirational wall-posters and aspirational intranet messages can't be replaced as a source of ethical conduct within an organization, it's your decisions as communication professionals that operationalize those goals. You bring those wall-posters to life. As one Chief Compliance Officer shared with me and her team, "we can all be a force for good each and every day in our work, in our decisions" if we all appreciate our role as gatekeepers to organizational ethics, culture and values. What an awesome if not daunting responsibility.

You, as an individual, along with your peers and mentors, are uniquely positioned to develop, guide and implement ethical messages internally and externally, as well as to push back when organizational objectives are not aligned with ethical and sustainable business practices. Even in conversations with business leaders, your opportunity to inspire and influence should not be undervalued or understated. And as Deirdre well shares, as a lesson I learned the hard way, if your organization is not serious about bringing 'poster values' to life through transparency in all communications, "this road of misalignment is not one you should choose to travel." But when your ethical DNA is aligned with your company's values, then you have a career replete with growth and opportunity, as you will be well positioned to amplify ethics and integrity, and to make sure they never get distorted, discarded or discounted in communications.

When I first started on my journey from corruption to compliance in 2014, terms like CSR (Corporate Social Responsibility) and ESG (Environmental, Social and Corporate Governance) were fringe topics in our world of ethics. Now they are drivers in multinational conduct, with multiple stakeholders, including investors, civil society and employees demanding transparency in how organizations are implementing these initiatives from the Board level down. And companies are being called to account when their communications are nothing but greenwashing, defined (Wikipedia) "as marketing spin in which green PR (green values) and green marketing are deceptively used to persuade the public that an organization's products, aims and policies are environmentally friendly and therefore 'better'." So, the personal and professional costs of being an ethical marketer in words but not deeds have never been greater. We have seen through the COVID-19 crisis how organizations have made 'lawful but awful' decisions, including the food processing and cruise-line industries. Not only those decisions, but how they were communicated, will be remembered long after the crisis has passed. Where were the ethical marketers in those organizations?

As Deirdre shares, "you take your brand character and persona with you wherever you go," to which I would add: guard it with your life. When your ethical DNA is misaligned with organizational conduct, you would be well advised to heed Deirdre's call for an "ethical mentor," to make certain that you are not compromising on an issue that will then go with you "wherever you go." As Deirdre will share in taking you through this journey, and as Warren Buffet well stated, "It takes 20 years to build a reputation and five minutes to ruin it." As communication professionals, you can be the guardian to make sure that those five minutes never occur by executing on your values, as gatekeepers to that reputation.

Remember, the pressure to succeed and the 'need for speed,' is going to be intense, but it's never too late, as Deirdre describes it, to "hit the pause button", to reach out to your mentor, and ask for help, to unpack your dilemma with your peers. Always embrace the idea that a license to succeed in your career is not a license to take a short cut, even if your peers are pressuring you to take one. I let the hazards of short-term thinking overwhelm what was in the long-term interest of society, my former employer, and most regrettably my family and health. I sacrificed ethics to succeed, but I didn't have to, and neither do you, ever.

Deirdre well shares, "I am yet to find the perfect marketer or business professional..." Agreed. I have had the honor of working with Volkswagen after their emissions scandal landed them in the crosshairs of multiple regulators. And as Hiltrud Werner shared in a press conference, it's not easy going from "shock to shame to change," yet for many of your organizations, you will be instrumental in helping your peers on that journey, as Deirdre helped me on mine. I agree with Deirdre's conclusion, "business utopia may be nowhere in sight." Values, ethics, and integrity will get challenged, but you, as an individual, and as part of what Deirdre describes as an "army of ethical people and champions who surround you," can make sure that those aspirational wall-posters come to life through everything you say and do, as "ethical marketers." So take a deep breath. My recommendation is to relax and read this book once, then take your supplies of highlighters and post-its and shine and memorialize what inspires you most. For me, it was, and is, everything!

By Richard Bistrong, CEO, Front-Line Anti-Bribery LLC

Introduction: The Journey to Ethics

A Personal Choice & Professional Practice

"We've overlooked a major safety issue. This is going to impact our customers and our bottom line. We're not exactly sure the extent of the damage yet. We're still assessing the situation," shared the company's Chief Operating Officer.

He continued, "It's important to take swift action and full responsibility. We have to be accountable for this unfortunate oversight. This means we'll need a full product recall."

"What's the best way to share the situation, and the potential damage? What are you thinking in terms of timing and how should we advise customers, media, employees and the public?" asked the CEO.

"We're still gathering the specifics from the product team and engineers. We should be able to inform our customers within the hour," stated their VP of communications. "At the same time, we have to show how we're correcting the oversight. This means action steps. What we will do to make everything 'right' including our plan moving forward. We need to assure everyone that this will **never** happen again," she further stated.

Why doesn't every company sound like this company? Why doesn't every team of executives act as quickly, ready for rapid response and the kind of transparent communication the public expects and needs? In this example, the executive team knows how maintaining trust and confidence in the market requires communication and critical action steps to help customers, and all their stakeholder groups, when missteps occur. They want to "right the wrong" quickly. When business professionals are faced with a "do-the-right-thing moment," why do some leaders make the wrong decisions?

Not every company, or every professional, will make the correct decision when faced with the pressures, challenges, and the important decisions they face. Mistakes and missteps will happen. There will be times when people do not realize the extent of the damage they are causing until the missteps play out publicly. Even the most informed (and well-intentioned) professionals are not free from errors or missteps in communication on behalf of their organizations.

However, the **difference** between honest mistakes, and the intentional misleading information shared with the public, often stems from the beliefs you have in place (your values) and the behavior or conduct that results. The ethics you practice are formed by your values and they play out in your decision-making, helping you to differentiate between right and wrong, good and bad, fair and unfair, and so on. These values guide you personally and professionally.

Who is the Ethical Marketer and what steps help a professional to carry the title? The Ethical Marketer will always embrace transparency as opposed to covering up a potentially harmful situation. They are honest, accurate and forthright with information. The Ethical Marketer wants to take responsibility and is accountable for situations and outcomes that are harmful or potentially harmful to the people they serve. They always have the best interest of customers and other stakeholder groups at heart. The Ethical Marketer is focused on helping the people who are affected by harmful actions, as the conduct relates to communication and their business. And the Ethical Marketer knows the importance of implementing action steps quickly to rectify a situation, especially one that negatively impacts the public. Most of all, ethical marketers learn from missteps, or the missteps of others, so as not to make the same mistake twice.

As an Ethical Marketer your ethics and good judgment are a crucial part of your decision-making in all your communication. When you practice ethics, you have an opportunity to maintain a positive brand reputation for your business and for yourself. But where does ethical behavior begin in the organization, and should the road to ethics and good judgment start with your company's leadership team, your HR department, or with you? There are two answers to this question. First, there is a co-responsibility of the leadership team, who are the senior role models, with the marketing and PR professionals, who create communications programs, along with the help of Human Resources to amplify the values and allow them to permeate every level and individual in an organization. They are all Ethical Marketers working together regardless of their individual titles in the company.

Now, for the second part. You, personally, should not wait to learn about ethics through your company or its ethical code of conduct and then adopt them as your own. For marketers and PR professionals (really, for any professional), ethics begin with your commitment to define personal values and what **you** stand for in your life and work. What are your personal values, and what influences your decision-making when you are communicating? Do ethics play out at the crossroads when you are challenged with tough decisions? Is it a "do no harm" decision-making process? Or a "harm the least number of people" thinking process? Have you taken the time to define your own ethics and values, so it is a lot easier to match them professionally to the role you play at your organization?

All that you value and that is important in your life become your ethical standards defined. You have been creating an ethics roadmap your entire life, which has to match your company's and what your organization expects from you. When personal and professional ethics align, there is helpful, meaningful, and valuable communication within the four walls of a firm and externally with the public. You see good judgment in decision-making play out at various touchpoints and in different interactions. You also see how the relationships within the organization and with external groups flourish. However, when there is a misalignment of ethics and values, there are communication challenges. You may face reputational risks, and credibility and integrity come into question. This road of mis-alignment is **not** one you should choose to travel and definitely a road to avoid at all costs.

A wise mentor once shared, "You **cannot** be a little bit ethical. You are either ethical or you are not." At the same time, the practice of ethics is not always viewed as personal or a choice of the heart, especially when it comes to your business communication. Why not? At the end of each day, professionals leave their companies and, in most cases, their work behind. However, what is left after the long business day is over? Either they walk away with their values and integrity intact, or they don't. There is no in between. No matter where or when you practice decision-making, your personal ethics go with you. Where your heart goes, your ethics and good judgment will follow.

With all the changes in technology, media and the communication land-scape, the journey to ethics has become more complicated. Years ago, the thought of "alternative facts" that misinform would have been laughed at in communications circles. There was no such label as "fake news." Artifi-cial Intelligence was not discussed widely as a threat to privacy or security. And bots on social media were not prevalent. Today, your personal and professional journey to ethics begins with a lot of questions and answers about technology, media, and information sharing.

Now you have a guide that delivers advice and stories from professionals who know what it means to face these changes, unforeseen challenges, and the ethical issues that surface when navigating a new landscape. *Answers for Ethical Marketers* is an easy Q&A book, which you can rely on to "gut check" your ethics against the advice and ethical standards of marketers and mentors, especially as you face challenges at different points in your career. Remember, the journey to ethics and good judgment are a personal choice and a professional practice.

Being an Ethical Marketer means you may encounter pressing decisions and your good judgment must prevail in situations that may not have existed in years past. When you face the changes in communications and in the media landscape, and what the public expects from you, good decision-making and ethical behavior must be the standard and the norm. How you approach ethics in communications will play out on your road to public confidence, showcasing the trust you instill and integrity you have worked so hard to build.

In Chapter 1, you will find the essentials and the ethical skills and practices that may fall outside of your traditional learning environment. The Q&A in this chapter offer a roadmap to better decisions when you are confronted with demanding situations. There are questions that surface around ethics every day. The advice, stories, and different ways to approach decision-making will help you as you experience the unexpected, as you live ethics in real time. The quick advice of a skilled professional, with a similar experience and a framework for good judgment, is there to guide you.

Chapter 2 offers answers to questions about how marketing through media channels has changed and shares some of the best practices for developing your company messages and stories for the public. What used to be a set number of larger channels with much longer news cycles has been replaced by the "long tail of media" and the speed of the Internet and social media. When unethical behavior and poor judgment play out through PR, digital marketing, and social media communications, the process to address these issues is no longer confined to specific channels and it can be near impossible to contain. Negative public sentiment spreads rapidly online and through social media communities. An ounce of prevention and ethics education goes a long way.

Chapter 3, Ethics in Cause Marketing, is another big area with the potential for communication missteps. Cause marketing can reap great rewards for professionals and their companies. However, the decision to give from the heart and to donate or work with a cause, in a new media landscape, has its ups and downs and a fair share of challenges. Your ethics must be front and center. Social media and all your social champions can be huge amplifiers of your cause. Of course, ethical missteps in cause marketing, which speaks to a deep lack of judgment, may have audiences less forgiving of your brand. The professionals who have engaged in cause marketing in the past may now find themselves in uncharted territory.

Ethics and good judgment go everywhere you go, especially to media interviews and appearances. The media has taken a beating in the ethics department and so have the professionals who are interviewed through broadcast channels, online media and blog outlets, podcasts, and livestreaming shows too. Because media is one of the quickest ways to get your message out, it is also a wake-up call for professionals to keep ethics in tow at all times. Chapter 4 addresses the questions and answers that marketers face as company executives share their thought leadership and lend a voice to important industry topics through media channels.

Chapter 5, Filtering Ethics Through Your Organization (beyond PR and marketing), shares advice focusing on the importance of building ethical champions throughout your company. Ethics may start with the PR people and your communications department. However, ethics penetrates every level and rank, especially the executives who need to walk the "ethics" talk. Now is the time to move from "we believe in our core values" written digitally and printed on the company walls to "we are a company practicing daily" and we stand by our ethics and good judgment. Practicing ethics at every touchpoint, including your internal communication with your employees, is a great starting point. After all, your employees are the gateway to your customers and other important stakeholder groups.

In Chapter 6, finding an ethical mentor can mean having a role model who is willing to share the stories and the personal situations you may not learn from the professionals in your organization. Mentors are more than happy to share the good, the bad, and the ugly of their ethics education. They are there to give you that subtle reminder about ethics; why it is important for professionals to take ethics seriously and with great pride. Because mentors are chosen carefully and with trust, your mentor will be the first one to let you know if and why a decision is a good one, or how it will lead to issues and ethics trouble. The mentors in Chapter 6 share their approach to ethical decision-making and their thought processes with you.

Leaders, it is time to listen up. Your employees are watching you closely. They will take your lead in the ethics department. There is no skimping here. If you are a leader, then doing what is best for the people around you has to come first. What your shareholders want most may be placed on the back burner. What makes an ethical leader and how do you place your ethics and good judgment above all else? The questions and answers in Chapter 7 demonstrate how leaders can take the lead and be responsible, and show their character as Ethical Marketers. At the same time, some situations will not always work out in perfect stakeholder harmony. However, valuable lessons are learned. If you want your people and your customers to thrive, then you will care deeply, and you will lead with ethics and values to guide you.

The last chapter in the book wraps up all of the questions and answers for Ethical Marketers, so that you can embrace the advice and shape your decision-making that plays out in all of your communications. As an Ethical Marketer, you also want to share the ethical experiences you believe will be important for your colleagues, team members or peers. *Answers for Ethical Marketers* will offer you a roadmap for guidance, tapping into your inner Ethics GPS, with a mentored approach to your decision-making. You will embark on new areas of consideration and ways to place your best ethical foot forward, as you better define, refine, or redefine your personal and professional ethics in your career.

Remember, defining, refining, and redefining ethics and values may start here. However, ethics and values do not and should not have to stop here. Ethical behavior in communications and business is an ongoing conversation, as consumers, technology, and media evolve and advance. So, get ready to define, refine or redefine your ethics and match them to your company's. Then you'll be on your way to navigating different situations, pressures and ethical challenges, which require your values and good judgment to show up and to always prevail.

If you are reading this book, then you understand the importance of ethics and you are ready to champion ethical marketing in all your communications and business interactions.

Chapter 1

Learning the Essentials & the Overarching Ethical Lessons

If someone asked you, "Can you define your values in 30-seconds or less?", would you be able to rattle them off quickly? Are your values engrained in your mind, in your heart, and are they a part of your everyday MO (Modus Operandi)? Defining your values is an exercise challenging you to identify your pillars of ethical conduct. Then, each pillar breaks down into the communication and the behavior you value, based on what is important to you personally, what you expect from yourself and from others around you.

Whether you realize it or not, your ethics and values also play out daily in your communications. They follow you down every conversation path and they are with you at every crossroad. Is it truth, accuracy, fairness, respect, objectivity, or is it all of the above that you hold as your ethical standards? Do you tell the truth and behave honestly and with integrity in your interactions? Do you focus on accuracy and do you stick with the facts? Are you able to listen without judgment and do you remain fair and objective? What about respect for others and where does your level of patience fall into your definition?

In many cases, professionals are first introduced to ethics in school, by learning about different situations and case studies. However, reading a textbook is not when the definition of ethics should be formed, or the point when you begin to practice ethics as an Ethical Marketer. Why not? Because ethics play out throughout your life. They are woven into situations you experience, both in your personal interactions as well as your career. What you value comes from your heart and has to make sense in your head. Your ethics and values are personal. Some call it a matter of the heart, reinforcing why it is important to think about, define clearly, and detail what you believe is ethical behavior long before you enter the workforce.

You may be saying, "I've already defined my values." Great news! You must also realize your values and ethical behavior are shaped and affected by different situations within your society and culture, family dynamics, friendships, your workplace, and the influential people around you. As much as you want to "say and do the right thing," alignment to your personal ethics can be challenged any day, and every day. Regardless of your age or experience, as these situations play out, you have the opportunity to either redefine or finetune your ethics. As you do, you will have a better understanding of yourself and what standards you will want to uphold as an Ethical Marketer.

If you have a set of ethics guiding you personally, then this book will help you to see how your life and career path coincide, as you adhere to your own standards. The Q&A in this chapter will help you to get to, or remain in, ethical alignment with stories, experiences, and examples to inform you and to also challenge the very basis of your ethics foundation.

Ethical behavior shows up in all your communications. It is your everyday standard, not just at work, it is wherever you go. As such, you need to be open, aware, and fully present with what matters the most to you. A commitment to these ethical standards helps you avoid compromising your integrity and character, as you face challenging situations in your life and work.

The Ethical Marketer has to rely on a strong foundation of ethics. Learning the essentials, on the road to ethics, is the best place to start.

Q1 How much are ethics personal vs. professional when you are communicating on behalf of a business?

Ethics do not stop at the door of your office building when you enter, and they do not stay at the office when you go home. If you are working remotely, then they do not turn on when you go online and turn off when you step away from your computer or smartphone.

For years, I have been saying who you are online is who you are in person and vice versa. You take your brand character and persona with you wherever you go. There are expectations of consistency and people expect you to act and communicate a certain way, no matter where you are and at every touch point with them. Your ethics are the thread that weaves through all your interactions, conversations, and marketing communications. Would you tell the truth to your friends and then lie to colleagues at work? Would you share news and information with complete transparency and accuracy on the job, yet embellish and use hyperbole with your family and friends? Chances are you will practice your ethics personally and professionally, and from your heart, at all times.

Ethics are reinforced in higher education. However, it is early in your childhood that you are introduced to and learn right from wrong. At a very early age you are watching your parents and role models and that is when your ethics begin to form. They become a part of your life and your DNA even before you recognize ethics as a part of your inner guidance system. Think of it as your Ethics GPS.[1] This same system of guidance gets honed, refined, and tested countlessly from your younger years all the way up until present day, and through the workday with all the communication you share.

Ethics are a personal choice with a professional alignment. You can't have one without the other. Ask yourself, is your Ethics GPS on all of the time?

Q2 What happens if my ethics do not match my company's?

I remember a challenging situation at my former marketing communications agency. We were a small growing agency with about 20 people. It was just after the 9/11 terrorist attack and our company was struggling with our marketing event business (large nationwide sales events) scaling back rapidly. Prior to the attack we had built a book of business focused on the creative development and production for several high-profile themed events. However, post-9/11, companies were traveling much less and not gathering their staff in major cities for large meetings. Clients cutting back took a large toll on our company and bottom line.

Around the same time, there was some excitement from my partners about work with a large conglomerate. I immediately pointed out that many of our clients were health related and children focused, and the conglomerate was not promoting the same health values and benefits. Working with this large corporation was not appealing and certainly did not excite me. This type of account was the antithesis of our work, which was more focused on people living healthy lives. As a matter of fact, working on the account did not interest me at all. The prospect of leading a team to benefit this organization challenged my ethics; the perfect example of my ethics in misalignment with my company's, at the time.

As a partner, I had one vote and I used it. However, there were other partners, so I was outvoted quickly. I made it known that I would steer clear of the sales pitch development and the meeting with the executives to safeguard my own values. At the end of the day, we did not win the business and my ethics remained intact.

There will be times when your ethics are challenged. My situation was business profit over ethical values. For me, it was important to place my values and the interests of our current clients first, which came down to trusting my Ethics GPS.

In the end, always let your good judgment guide you to your higher standards.

Q3 Does Emotional Intelligence (EI) affect ethical behavior?

Absolutely! Your level of EI can be proportionate to your ethical behavior. Here's why you want to increase your EI for better judgment in your decision-making. Think about the communication at your company and on social media during a time of issues or crisis. At these times, would you expect to see a lot of emotional intelligence? How can you tell. Here is a quick quiz to evaluate your level of EI:

- Do you respond rather than react? (Example: Listening without judgment)
- Do you practice self-control? (Example: Your level of present, calm and focused participation)
- Do you exercise self-awareness? (Example: Ability to see both sides of an issue)
- Do you adapt well to change? (Example: Your ability to course correct quickly)
- Do you serve the needs of others? (Example: Your ability to help others succeed)

Based on the answers to these questions, if you answered "yes" with confidence to each question, then you are practicing emotional intelligence. When you show self-awareness, exhibit self-control, and reserve judgment, you are much more likely to you have a "check" on your own behavior.

The definition of emotional intelligence describes the need to manage your own actions and reactions (your behavior first). When you do this successfully, you are able to be more aware and to manage the behaviors of others. Being more aware of how you come across, also helps you to listen, process, and tune into someone else's situation more accurately. EI helps you to make a more informed decision with a true understanding as opposed to a knee-jerk reaction that leads to a poorly guided decision.

With more emotional intelligence, your decisions will come from a place of knowledge and keen perception, and the resulting communication will ultimately serve and be beneficial to others.[2]

Q4 What do you do when you are asked to flat-out lie?

One of my early mentors was very clear about lying. He said, "Lying is a relationship ender and a deal breaker." The words "do not lie" have always stuck in my head. Public Relations Strategist, Fraser Seitel, has been practicing Public Relations for decades. He is the President of Emerald Partners and has been named among the 100 most distinguished professionals in the PR industry. I have used Fraser's book, *The Practice of Public Relations*, in my NYU and UMASS at Amherst classes for years. The chapter on ethics is one that should be read by students and reread by all professionals.[3]

After using Fraser's book and studying his work in my classes, many of my students would question, "Why would anyone think lying is a good idea?" It is a logical question. Why would you lie for yourself or for anyone else? Of course, the pressures of your work and a business situation might lead to a poor judgment and a negative outcome. However, whether it is lying to your employees, customers, the media, shareholders, partners, or any important constituent, lies cause harm and pain, and they place your credibility in severe jeopardy. It can take years to build trust, which can be lost in an instant, without the chance of ever gaining back that trust. Whether you realize it or not, technology and social media has everyone operating in a type of "fishbowl" environment. Eventually, the truth will come out and then it will follow you around.

If you are still on the fence about lies being a relationship ender and a deal breaker (even the little "white lies"), ask yourself, "How did you feel the last time someone lied to you?" Did you want to forge a deeper relationship with that person? Did you rush to include them in your business deals or hire them as a partner or seek her out as your go-to resource?

Chances are you will move on to a new contact or a more trustworthy colleague who has been a reliable and credible professional. One more reminder here: Do Not Lie.

Q5 What do you do if you're asked to shift the blame for wrongdoing to someone else?

When the news came out regarding Wells Fargo setting up fake accounts for its customers, they did not take accountability. Blaming your employees, customers, or anyone for your unethical behavior, is never a good idea. The Ethics 101 Manual says you need to own up to your mistakes and to take responsibility for your actions. Of course, you would expect the CEO, a seasoned leader and role model, of one of the largest banks in the world to own up to corporate fraud. However, taking responsibility was not the desired approach at the time. Instead, the bank's early explanation for the alleged illegal sales practice was to throw their employees under the bus.[4]

Was it their compensation program, a lack of compliance, or was it the pressure from management to reach a certain number of new accounts, a quota, if you will? The CEO defended his company. He shared with the news media that there was no incentive for any of their salespeople to have this type of reasoning for the behavior. Wells Fargo didn't give their people any incentive to "do bad things." Yet, it happened, and this is how the conduct was explained.[5]

Why does anyone shift the blame knowing they will pay the price later? Wells Fargo was eventually fined and agreed to pay $3 billion to settle their charges for fraudulent sales practices. They also acknowledged collecting fees for products their customers never agreed to have and, quite frankly, did not need.

Is it a lack of clarity on the situation? Is there conscious unethical behavior going on and shifting the blame is a way to say, "Look over here?" which never works out well.

Ethical Marketers (remember as a spokesperson, the CEO is the head Ethical Marketer) use the Dale Carnegie approach. Rather than letting ego, fear, or just downright hubris get in your way, it is time to ask some questions. In Carnegie's book, *How to Stop Worrying and Start Living*, he posed this question, "What is the worst-case scenario [the worst that can happen]?"[6] In this case it was a $3 billion fine which they had to pay anyway. The CEO should have gotten to the bottom of the allegations quicker, saving precious time, and reputation damage.[7]

Facing and moving through the worst that can happen sooner is a step toward reputation repair. In the end, 5,300 employees were released, and the sales quotas were discontinued. Shifting the blame delays the course correction, which further adds to the reputation damage, both in opinion and financial reparations.

Q6 What do I do if I know a decision is unethical and speaking up means I'll lose my job?

When you walk through the New York City subways, the MTA posts signs that say, "If you see something, say something."

If you saw something that was potentially harmful in the subway would you just walk by or would you alert the authorities? What would your ethics and values tell you to do? It's a similar principle that has to be visited, at times, at your company. If you see or hear something that makes you take pause, or you know information will be shared that is harmful, would you question it, or would you just do what you are told?

Questioning and doing what you are told actually varies by generation. Here's the good news, Generation Z (Gen Zers) are known as a generation that questions before they do what they are told. Working with bright interns, I like to say they are personally programmed to ask questions. Let me give you an example. I was working on a project for a client. The client's team was made up of Gen X, millennials and an intern, who was our lone Gen Zer.

After the team mapped out the strategy, it was refreshing (and pleasantly surprising) to have the intern send an email to the team questioning the timing of her task. She pointed out the timing looked off and the team should take a closer look and explain why they were implementing a tactic that seemed premature. In her estimation, what was about to be shared was inaccurate based on the timing. Accuracy is an important standard to uphold in communications. How did the team miss this?

Here is the lesson: If you see something, say something. Of course, the error was an inadvertent oversight. In this case, speaking up was easier with leeway in the planning. When you are not under intense pressure, and there is no looming crisis with the media knocking down your door, saying something comes without question.

Yet, it is immensely important to take a pause and ask a question when you are under intense pressure, even if it means compromising the security of your position. Now, that may seem harsh and sounds near impossible whether you are young and finding your way in your career, or you are a seasoned pro with a family to feed. However, if you do not say something, then what plays out could be a number of scenarios that will jeopardize your position anyway.

Whatever misinformation is shared or lies and cover up occur, anyone involved is at risk. At least by opening up, questioning and asking others, the decision-making is not left in your hands. It takes a collective group of Ethical Marketers to reinforce ethical standards and to steer toward good judgment.

At the end of the day, you can rise together or fall together. What you question in between may just be the determining factor.

Q7 Is there a way to challenge unethical communication before it is shared?

Unethical communication can only be challenged if you and the people around you realize the communication is unethical. Having your ethics and values defined going into a situation is only half the battle. The other half is having the good sense with your peers to pause or even stop completely, re-evaluate, process, and come to the conclusion that there is a better way to communicate.

Years ago, I worked with Richard Bistrong who you have already met in the Foreword of this book. Today, he is the CEO of Front-Line Anti-Bribery LLC. When I first met Richard, he was just out of prison after being incarcerated for violating FCPA and Anti-Bribery laws. Richard reached out to me, having read my book, *Putting the Public Back in Public Relations*. He wanted me to help him to rebuild his reputation and to assist in sharing a new story and trajectory to educate business professionals about the importance of being compliant and making the right choices at their companies. Today, Richard's goal is to inspire leaders to discuss and mitigate the challenges of international business. He uses his personal journey "to raise awareness and sensitivity with respect to ethical decision making."[8]

When Richard and I shared the stage at the Florida Public Relations Association's annual conference I remember he discussed how many of his international sales deals were done alone in countries around the world. After making several choices, which led to an FBI investigation and cooperating with US and UK law enforcement for approximately five years, Richard realized how involving other people would have helped him to make different and better choices.

When you can open up a potential decision, or your intended action with others on your team or in your network, you can use the wisdom of your peers. They can "gut check" their ethical standards or Ethics GPS against yours. Group alignment on a decision is a much better way to determine if you are moving forward with good intentions or if you are headed down a road of potential trouble.

One way to challenge unethical communication or actions is to avoid making choices alone.

Q8 What is the best way to spread ethical decision-making among your peers?

Trying to spread ethical decision making when a tough situation is playing out, or you are on a tight deadline for a campaign, is not the time to be contemplating the ethics education at your firm. How you spread ethical standards, and have people adopt communication values, must be embraced long beforehand. The key to ethics success in your company is to educate early, update regularly as new situations are evaluated, and offer easy access to resources for all company employees to review and support.

There is no excuse for an organization not having ethics built into the company's structure and culture. With all of the industry resources available (Codes of Ethics from different organizations to YouTube videos on the subject), at the very least ethics can be a part of the HR onboarding process, with reading material in a resource center. I wish I could confirm with 100% confidence that 100% of US companies spell out ethical standards in their employee handbooks or somewhere in their corporate materials. It may also be a stretch to say, with the same confidence, they offer mandatory ethics interval training, whether it is online or through in-person workshops. Unfortunately, I don't have the statistics, and can only speculate the percentage is less than 100%.

Today, employees will be challenged with different situations. Why would companies want their employees to learn the hard way and in real-time? Instead, having a process in place for evaluating and documenting ethical practices from past situations is a much better approach. Your employees can learn through the experience of their peers and past predecessors.

Spreading ethical decision-making among your peers comes down to good education (how ethics and values are spelled out) and role modeling (the action). It is a lot easier to have people realize what is and what is not ethical and exercise good judgment in their communication, if it is a part of their positive work experience and your company's workplace culture. The ideal situation is to learn from peers and leaders who are role modeling the good decision-making whether they are, or they are not in the thick of a crisis situation.

Q9 Who is responsible for unethical communication, the person sharing the information or the source of origination?

I have heard on countless occasions, "He asked me to do something. So, I did what I was told" and "I was just following a directive." It happens all the time. Does this make the person who follows through with the poor judgment responsible? It really depends on a few factors. Experience plays a part in the process, especially if the employee is new to the company or has just entered the workforce.

Grabbing the intern or first year entry-level employee who has very little business or real-world PR and marketing experience and asking them to do something that you know is wrong is troublesome on many fronts. Here are two reasons to consider.

First, the intern is not familiar with the normal process of communication or the business. Having insights into formal protocol is not something that is or should be expected. It is only through experience that new professionals are able to make an ethical choice because they have an understanding or can contrast what is the right way to proceed and what might be unethical steps.

Unfortunately, everyone involved in a questionable incident or misleading communication distributed by a company faces the consequences. And, yes, there are always consequences. The difference here is that acting with malicious intent is different than not having the experience to know you are actually getting wrapped up in these harmful actions.

Second, interns or young professionals are not prepared to "speak truth to power" because they are at a lower, more vulnerable level and they feel their position will "be on the line." They are not skilled at an approach that allows them to question or present information that is contrary to what the executive or manager expects. Being able to open a conversation with "I have some new or different insights for you, so please keep an open mind as this may change the course of our communication approach and the impact you were looking to achieve," is highly unlikely.

One of my earlier career experiences falls into the "She asked me do something, so I did it," category. I shared a story in my book, *Answers for Modern Communicators*, about speaking truth to power. At the time, I was a young professional and was not able to rise to the occasion. My Vice President (VP) asked me to deliver a letter directly to a client by hand. As I was leaving to hand-deliver the envelope, my direct supervisor told me I did not have to personally deliver anything and because the envelope was addressed, I could stick it in the mail with the proper postage.[9]

My supervisor told me that I was needed at the office and that everyone agreed this was the best approach. So, I took the elevator to the lobby and stuck the envelope in the mail slot. As I turned around, there was my VP, quite upset that I had not followed her directive.

Speaking truth to power would have meant me standing up to my supervisor and saying, "I'm happy to help here. However, I'll be mentioning to our VP the change in plans." Or, getting both parties in the room together to let them decide the right course of action would have also been a good option here.

Ultimately, I played a part in a potentially damaging situation when a letter was not hand delivered to the client in a timely fashion. I was responsible, yet my inexperience was not held against me. In fact, it taught me to ask more questions and to always make sure everyone was on the same page when important decisions about client communication needed to be made.

Q10 What are some additional resources to guide a personal and professional ethics journey?

I have my favorite personal resources, although this is not an exhaustive list. A simple Google search, or even searching in your social media communities, will give you numerous resources on ethics education. Asking peers and colleagues and other business professionals is one of the best ways to find the resources that are the most helpful. Crowdsourcing, whether it is on a blog, Twitter, LinkedIn or Facebook, will also offer up any number of trusted sources.

When searching and crowdsourcing, here are three organizations that all have a detailed Code of Ethics or have a Code of Ethical Conduct.

- **The Public Relations Society of America (PRSA) Code of Ethics.** You do not have to be a member of PRSA to access their Code of Ethics, which is available on the organization's website. The ethics area is comprehensive with downloadable case studies relating to professional conduct and content issues, as well as digital issues and organizational issues to avoid. In addition, professionals can access an ethics quiz to test their ethical choices and an ethics on-demand webinar.[10]
- **The American Marketing Association (AMA) Statement of Ethics.** The AMA dedicates an area of their website to ethical conduct, which includes a Statement of Ethics, ethical norms, and a detailed breakdown on ethical values and implementation of these professional standards. The AMA expressly states, "As marketers, we recognize that we not only serve our organizations but also act as stewards of society in creating, facilitating and executing the transactions that are part of the greater economy."[11]
- **International Association of Business Communicators (IABC) Professional Conduct.** The IABC wants its members to know that they have a responsibility to society through the delivery of communication that has "the potential to influence economies and affect lives." Their Code of Ethics stands as a guide for both personal and professional conduct.

Members of IABC are required to sign an ethical conduct statement and have access to resources and assistance through an Ethics Committee.[12]

Please, do not stop here with these professional resources. One simple "ask" on Facebook, LinkedIn or Twitter will deliver a number of peer and crowd-sourced options to help you.

Q11 Why do some companies have "problem areas" in marketing that lead to unethical communication?

All companies have potential ethical problem areas. If you were to start with your marketing and PR department, do you know where these problem areas exist? If you do not have an answer to this question, or you are naming issues that you "think" are problem areas, then it is time to take a much closer look.

Communication flows in and out of these departments regularly, whether you have a large, medium or small company. You have to set the stage and make marketing the model or best practice standard before you roll out what "problem free" looks like for the rest of the organization. You may be asking, "Where do I start?" Good communication begins with an understanding of where you have been, why the communication has benefitted customers and constituents, or if it has had the opposite effect on important stakeholders.

Although auditing your communication is an in-depth exercise, here are a few starter questions to get the process going and to uncover those underlying and potentially damaging issues and areas that need more or tighter ethical guidelines:

- Are deadlines for campaigns and marketing programs reasonable or are they rushed where miscommunication is frequently distributed?
- What kind of checks and balances do you have on your campaigns or program materials? How many professionals are involved in the approval process?
- What kind of training or materials are available to your marketing team, if they have questions about communication that comes out of marketing and PR departments?
- What are the frequent communication bottlenecks and are these areas contributing to a lack of accuracy, transparency, fairness, etc., in your communications?
- What kind of resources are available to your marketing and PR team to check and double-check facts, figures, data, accuracy, etc., in your communications? Does fact-checking go beyond your team's knowledge and insights?

- What kind of documentation exists for communication that is unsuccessful and yes, at times leads to issues for your company?

If you audit your communication programs beginning with these questions, then you will be well on your way to identifying where communication issues may bubble up and potentially cause ethical problems when the communication is released. Realizing you may need new parameters, guidelines, resources, additional timing, and different processes are the start to eradicating the problem areas in your firm.

Q12 Is PR the most poised to handle and respond the ethical issues?

Asking a PR person this question will surely draw the answer, "yes." When you are a trained and experienced professional you are a skilled relationship builder who develops the bridges between an organization and its public(s). With any strategic relationship comes trust, integrity, independence, fairness, the safeguarding of information, and avoiding any conflicts of interest.

A great deal of the value of the company communication and the work of the PR team come down to public opinion and confidence. However, because the public is grappling with thousands of messages through all of their channels and a news cycle that is fast and furious, a company's ethics through its communicators is prominently displayed and in the spotlight for all to see.

However, what would have brought scandalous headlines years ago, could come and go so quickly. Fact-checking, in the era of the Trump Administration, is nearly impossible and hyperbole and sarcasm, as well as "he was only joking" come out of the Office of the President.[13] Yes, times certainly have changed and politicians, and press secretaries, as well as the journalists reporting the news, are not seen in the most favorable light.

So, who does the public believe? Are the people who tell you everything you want to hear the people that you will ultimately trust? Or is it the people who tell you what you **need** to know, even if it is not always pleasant, who you rely on and hold in a positive light? Are these the people who you find credible? If you think it is the latter, then you are in the Ethical Marketer camp. In my experience, when you are hearing what you need to hear in a timely fashion, there is a PR team behind the transparent communications in a "do the right thing" moment.

According to the Edelman Trust Barometer, companies did better in 2019, when the study reported that "my employer" has emerged globally as the most trusted institution, at 75%. At the same time, government and the media were trusted 48% and 47%, respectively. When "my employer" or businesses and NGOs are seen as more favorable trusted sources, in most cases, I would like to believe that PR people are helping with the filling up of the public "cup" of good will.[14]

In most organizations, when PR drives the communication, it has a megaphone and these professionals know the value of authentic and transparent communications. Most PR professionals have a code of ethics through their associations and take this oath of ethical conduct seriously. They reinforce these ethic and values through their work as reliable, accurate, objective and trusted resources. As Ethical Marketers, they have the ear of the CEO and are known to be the tied closely to the state of the brand's health and reputation.

If you want to know whether a company's public cup of goodwill is halfway full or halfway empty, then just ask a PR professional. Their role is to continually use research, strategy, and planning to produce communication which upholds ethical standards and good judgment and keeps the trust and the cup of goodwill filled to the brim.

Q13 What is the best ethics advice you have ever received?

As a young PR professional, I learned to listen carefully, ask more questions, and to trust my instincts. When you are early in your career or even if you're under intense pressure or stress, this is not always easy. Under these situations, the opposite is true. You may be doubting yourself and not listening to the little voice (your inner Ethics GPS) that is putting up the red flags as you are going down the wrong path.

One of my early mentors would always remind me to use my Eagle Eyes and to be inquisitive. In other words, listen closely and then have your eyes and ears wide open to catch what should not go out of our company. I remember wearing the moniker "Eagle Eyes" as a badge of honor. This didn't always mean that I was able to avoid every misstep. I have made plenty. However, if I did anything that showed poor judgment unintentionally, then there was on opportunity to step back to re-evaluate what an Eagle Eye would have done and what questions should have been asked.

Asking questions is a practice that should be adopted early on and used throughout your career. Leaders listen closely and ask many questions. They want to explore all angles. They want to hear many different options available and then trust their gut instincts and Ethics GPS. By asking questions you are also pausing, slowing down the knee-jerk reaction and/or refraining from using an ego option, or selecting an option based on what your ego tells you. If you lead with your ego, you're starting in a defensive position rather than an offensive one.

The best advice that I share with you: Listen closely, be an Eagle Eye and ask a lot of questions. Use your ears and eyes to uncover different perspectives that will help to guide you. Also, remember that you do not have to fly alone.

The Marketing Experts "Weigh In" on Ethical Guidance

Four Signposts for Ethical Communications

By Rebekah Iliff, founder of WriteVest

Why should communication professionals, content creators, and marketers consider ethics important when, by today's standards, it seems like leaders and people in power positions bend every rule in the book in order to "win?" Perhaps this is simply the perception and not the reality. Maybe "opinionators" committing politics and engaging in shouting matches on national news syndicates is an illusion. Furthermore, isn't "fake news" just something people say to obfuscate valid points?

When considering how often the powers-that-be conflate ethical violations with freedom of speech, it's no wonder being a professional communicator can have us questioning what's objectively appropriate and likely (and ultimately) best for business. In other words, how do we "do what they say, not what they do" when it comes to ethical communication.

In order to keep myself (and my teams) in check, I've tried to root my decision-making in a handful of useful signposts during my 20 years as a communications pro—both as an internal executive and a client-facing business owner. Using these signposts as a litmus test for ethical behavior certainly hasn't made me rich or powerful (yet!), but I can sleep at night with my integrity intact. Beyond that, I haven't had to play the game of "covering my tracks." Who has time for that anyway? Lying publicly, or even internally, to save face or come out ahead is always a losing game—eventually.

SIGNPOST #1: PRIMUM NON NOCERE, OR "FIRST, DO NO HARM."

This concept originated from the ancient Greek physician, Hippocrates, and is grounded in the belief that "given an existing problem, it may be better not to do something (or even do nothing) than to risk causing more harm than good." This maxim is a core tenet of the healthcare profession, when the result of a specific decision could be death. Imagine if communicators—including journalists and public-facing figures entrusted with information sharing—used this maxim? They may not, but you'd probably be wise to do so. In the very least, having this burned into your brain will give you pause before you press "Tweet" on that questionable fact sourced from a 13-year-old's TikTok account.

SIGNPOST #2: KARMA SCHOOL OF BUSINESS.

While we often don't see the negative repercussions of other people's poor decisions, the karmic principle is airtight. Maybe the narcissistic, megalomaniac billionaire never gets hauled off to jail or loses his riches in a stock market crash, but does he or she have any real friends? It may be convenient to appease your boss by bending the truth in order to get that story splashed all over the front page of *The New York Times*, but you may just lose your job as a result if the leadership needs a scapegoat. Err on the side of playing it straight to avoid the consequences later. Plus, behaving like a true pro will eschew that nagging guilt and those pesky, negative voices. Consider choosing the ethical approach as a pre-emptive strike against chronic self-hatred.

SIGNPOST #3: GRANDPARENTS SPECTRUM OF DISAPPOINTMENT.

In 1998, during a sub-par modeling job,* the photographer told me I should consider posing for *Playboy Magazine* (in those days it was print only). I was simultaneously flummoxed and flattered before putting him in his place with the best retort that came to mind: "My rule of thumb for modeling is that I won't ever do anything that may horrify my sweet, Southern, German-Lutheran grandparents." Tasteful lingerie for a retail catalog? Sure. But that was my limit. He shrugged and, to his credit, didn't try to convince me otherwise. Since that incident, I've attempted to make decisions based on "the grandparents' spectrum of disappointment." While they are no longer living, when faced with a difficult, ethical dilemma, I still weigh my decisions based on the spectrum. If I think they would have been even slightly horrified, if possible, I choose another way.

I was 19, and this was before I began my career as a writer, communication, and marketing pro. I was also super poor, so turning down a potential magazine job wasn't easy. All I'm saying is, in retrospect, I'm grateful for my staunch Lutheran grandparents. I'm also grateful there was no Internet, YouTube, Twitter, Snap, Facebook, or other photo sharing viral platforms because I may not have a job right now.

SIGNPOST #4: DON'T TALK ABOUT IT, BE ABOUT IT.

This one may seem antithetical to communicators, but ethics are less about what you decide to communicate and more about how you operate and behave as a professional. We all know the guy or gal who talks a big game, then under pressure caves at the first sign of controversy or confrontation. People will respect the way that you act when faced with challenges, but they won't respect you if talking is the only thing you do. Remember that not saying something—or silence—can sometimes be the best option; as long as you are doing your best to make ethical choices in all that you do. Stand for something, stand up for others, and stand your ground when it comes to being someone YOU can live with. The rest falls into place.

Integrity is Your Biggest Asset

By Corina Manea, Digital Marketer, Brand Strategist and Blogger

Integrity has been part of my personal and professional journey ever since I can remember. My guiding principle and motto have always been "treat others how you'd like to be treated." When you put this lens to everything you do in both business and personal life, your outlook on life changes dramatically. Business becomes about what you can do for your clients, how can you help them more. You become part of their struggles and successes.

Sometimes it's hard. Sometimes you're pressured to take the shortcut because there is too much at stake! At least that's what you're told, or even you tell yourself. However stressful some moments can be, let's keep in mind they are just that, moments.

When you feel pressured, when you feel like everyone wants a "piece of you," take a step back and look at the big picture. Put things in perspective. What's the worst thing that can happen if you follow your gut and principles? Lose your job? Lose the client? Be admonished by your boss?

Once you answer these questions and you feel like your blood pressure is through the roof and anxiety kicks in, think of a moment in your life that was way harder than what's happening right now. How did you overcome it? What did you do to get back on your feet? Retrace the steps you took back then. Feel the confidence you gained as you worked your way through it and how did it feel to get to the other side successfully.

You did it, no one else. You can do it again, and again, and again.

Now look at what's happening right now? Does it still feel like it's the end of the world? It doesn't, does it?

We spend most of our time inside our heads, analyzing and over analyzing, playing worse-case scenarios and becoming overwhelmed by fear. When you're able to put things in perspective, to remember you are a powerful human being who's overcome more than what's going on in a particular moment, you get that detachment needed to make the right decision. While losing a job or a client are not happy circumstances, they are replaceable. However, when you betray your own integrity and ethics, you have to live with those decisions and feelings of guilt all your life.

Here's the funny thing. To earn your customers' trust, you have to put ethics first. Integrity is your bigger asset, whether you know it or not. When you realize that and start leading a life full of integrity, all things fall into place. People will reach out to you because they know you are trustworthy, because they know you'll make the right decisions no matter what.

But how do you stay connected to your values in the noisy world we live in? It starts with authenticity and being true to yourself. People will always respond positively if you are sincere. And let me be clear, it's not always easy to be honest and open. But it pays off in the long run.

Transparency is essential in business and life. Always be willing to share information that helps others. It's the starting point of building meaningful relationships with everyone, your clients, colleagues, social media communities. You want to become the first person who comes to mind when they have a question. You become their trusted source.

Honoring your commitments is part of your integrity and ethical behavior. Do what you promised you would. And if something comes up that requires your full attention and doesn't allow you to follow through on a promise, let people know. And most importantly, don't wait until the last moment to say something. Your credibility will diminish, and it will be very hard for you to get it back. Keep your word and you'll be amazed how people will come to you.

Put yourself in the other person's shoes. Empathy opens the doors to true communication and authentic relationships. If you want to become your clients' trusted advisor, put yourself in their shoes. Before recommending them a course of action, take a minute to really listen to them. How would you feel if you were them? What would you do? Spend some time considering their options and, once you've done that, take the time to explain to them your recommendations; why you believe that's the best course of action and how it will help them.

Kindness and respect are paramount in being an ethical marketer. In a world where everyone is focused on reaction, take the time to think through before you respond. You never know what your clients, people in your community or even a stranger on the street are going through. They may be having a hard time. They may be going through something you can't even imagine. Treat everyone with kindness and respect. And if you can't help them in any way, just give them your kind words. They'll probably need to hear them. When you're kind to others, you will attract people who treat you kindly and with respect in business and in your personal life.

Be honest, be transparent, keep your word, put yourself in the other person's shoes and be kind. These timeless principles are as true today as ever and they can guide you to become the best person and marketer you can be.

Ethics and Values Define Us

By Wendy Glavin, CEO, Wendy Glavin Agency, Equities Contributor

My father, a prosecutor, was my role model. Although he passed 18 years ago, his life lessons are ingrained in me. I remember him telling me that, "If the city clerk doesn't file my case, I can't go to court; even though I'm a partner, we're all equal."

Another example is that the attorneys had to wear suits and ties on the sixth floor and throughout the firm. The support staff was required to work on the fourth floor only. Whenever my father went to the fourth floor, he removed his jacket to illustrate equality.

To me, ethics and values are a part of us and define who we are. After working for 30 years in marketing communications, whether I'm speaking to friends, colleagues, or clients, my moral code is the same: to be honest, to act with integrity, to be trustworthy, loyal, fair, caring, responsible for my own actions, and to advocate for others.

Since I'm always honest, I don't tell people what they want to hear. People either choose to hire me or not, but I always stay true to my values. One of my favorite books is Adam Grant's *Originals: How Non-Conformists Move the World*.

In Grant's book, he discusses how to identify great ideas, why we need to speak up, and how leaders can build cultures that welcome dissent for more creative problem-solving. He shares how an image of the founders are built into companies along with differing perspectives. I completely agree.

Grant suggests, "If you only hire people who fit your values and business model, you're going to end up breeding groupthink and losing diversity of thought. You need originals to keep bringing fresh ideas that can challenge your current business model, your assumption, and your principles."[15]

Often, people are afraid to speak up out of a fear of being wrong or don't like taking risks. Going through life without bringing our whole selves to our work is a competitive disadvantage. Even if it means losing our job or clients, it's better than feeling undervalued, unappreciated, or taken for granted.

My father used to tell me, if you're not accepted at a college it means it's not the right fit. The same applies to our work and relationships. Trust your gut. If you have an interview, reflect on the conversation, and how it made you feel. Or, if you're speaking with a prospective client, make sure you listen to how they're speaking to you. If you don't feel that the relationship will be a collaborative one, it's better to walk away and end on a positive note.

Generally speaking, those of us who are advocates for our clients, the relationships we build, and the ideas we share, tend to over-deliver. Several years ago, a blockchain start-up hired me to write and edit their website, whitepaper, and pitch decks. The client lived outside the US and was only in New York City for three months. Since I wanted the client to be successful, I continued working and accruing additional hours, for which he could not compensate me. The outcome was a great learning experience for me about setting boundaries and limits, so all involved realized the value.

In this situation, I reflected on my emotions to help guide my thinking and behavior. It was emotional intelligence (EI) that allowed me to look through a different lens. Once we get to the root of how we feel and react, it helps us to avoid or solve problems before they arise. Some people believe that EI is innate, however, we can learn by bringing our whole selves to work. This means being authentic, vulnerable, and leading with humility to create deeper and more meaningful relationships.

My dream was to become a lawyer, but my father said, "To win your case, you need to see the other side; you're more of an advocate." Now, years later, I can see the other side. It takes practice but it is like looking into a crystal ball and understanding where the other person is coming from. It has helped me stick to my moral code and to improve my relationships with my three grown boys, friends, colleagues, and clients too.

Notes

1 Ethics GPS is a term used to highlight how you can use your inner instincts or "gut" reactions to guide your ethical conduct.
2 Bernard Knight, "Six Core Values and Five Emotional Intelligence Skills Leading to Sound Ethical Decisions," IP Watchdog Blog, July 2017.
3 Fraser Seitel, *The Practice of Public Relations*, Chapter 6 Ethics, Pearson, February 2016.
4 Adam K. Raymond, "Wells Fargo CEO Blames Massive Fraud Scheme on its Employees," New York Magazine, September 2016.
5 Emily Glazer and Christina Rexrode, "Wells Fargo CEO Defends Bank Culture, Lays Blame with Bad Employees," Wall Street Journal, September 2016.
6 Dale Carnegie, *How to Stop Worrying and Start Living*, Gallery Books, p. 15, October 2004.
7 Scott Horsley, "Wells Fargo Paying $3 Billion to Settle U.S. Case Over Fraudulent Customer Accounts," NPR, February 2020.
8 Richard Bistrong Website, https://richardbistrong.com/about, December 2020.
9 Deirdre Breakenridge, *Answers for Modern Communicators*, Routledge, p. 63, October 2017.
10 Public Relations Society of America, Code of Ethics, https://www.prsa.org/about/ethics.
11 American Marketing Association, Codes of Conduct/AMA Statement of Ethics, https://www.ama.org/codes-of-conduct.
12 International Association of Business Communicators, IABC Code of Ethics for Professional Communicators, https://www.iabc.com/about-us/purpose/code-of-ethics.
13 John Harwood, "Trump's Favorite Tools—Hyperbole and Exaggeration—Turn into Traps," CNBC, https://www.cnbc.com/2017/05/17/trumps-favorite-tools-hyperbole-and-exaggeration-turn-into-traps.html, May 2017.
14 Edelman Trust Barometer, News & Awards, "Return to the Largest-Ever Inequality of Trust Driven By Spike Among Informed Public," https://www.edelman.com/news-awards/2019-edelman-trust-barometer-reveals-my-employer-most-trusted-institution#, January 2019.
15 Adam Grant, *Originals: How Non-Conformists Move the World*, WH Allen, p. 179, February 2016.

Chapter 2

Applying Ethics Through All Your Media Channels

Perhaps you have considered your PR and communications department as the "ethical brain" of your organization. Typically, the role of the public relations professional is that of "Brand Police Officer" maintaining and protecting your brand reputation.[1] Yes, as you may know, I am a PR person (and a marketer too) and I have carried this label proudly. PR professionals are trained in ethics. They are known for listening and responding to what is shared publicly about a company or its brand products especially when issues or crisis occur. As reputation managers, being a watchful eye certainly falls within our purview and becomes an automatic and often unquestioned responsibility. PR also helps to set the tone and voice for the company, speaks to the character and integrity of the organization, and guides the professionals who communicate with the public.

However, PR cannot be the ethical brain alone. Marketing is also there, creating the stories and messaging to drive leads and sales through creative content and storytelling. Collectively, these Ethical Marketers, can plant the seeds that have the potential to penetrate the rest of the organization. Of course, right along with them will be their leaders and role models championing values and the ethical behavior, with the HR department helping with the policies to support their efforts. We will take a good look at leadership and ethics in Chapter 7. With all of the communication flowing through your channels, have you identified where ethical communication begins with your team?

With the speed of social media and the Internet, it is better to identify and coalesce this core communications team sooner rather than later. Your team of Ethical Marketers should capitalize on the mix of PR and marketing experience in your company. Your Ethical Marketers know the media and your communications process. They can take the deep dive into the guidelines, guardrails and ethical standards, which should be in place for your programs. Digging into ethics in communications means uncovering the ways in which accepted values drive the decision-making process, which leads to the news, content, and stories that flow through your channels. The team may quickly identify the situations where good judgment in communication is blocked, and where the potential problem areas tend to surface. Ethical Marketers look at the big picture; a holistic view of the marketing content to be shared. You are also deeming the content acceptable for others to propagate as well.

Today, with a mix of media available in the PESO model, which is Paid, Earned, Shared and Owned media, you have a lot of ethical filtering and good judgment to apply, before releasing any communication.[2] Ethical concerns can also grow as media channels change and so does the technology you use to create and share your company stories and messages. What used to be a set number of larger channels with longer news cycles have been replaced by the long tail of media, and the speed of the Internet and social media. Unfortunately, when poor judgment plays out through any channel, the process to address issues is no longer confined to that specific channel. Instead, social media has become a conduit to negative and also the "fake news" that can be impossible to contain.

There will always be unethical behaviors beyond your control, on the Internet and in social media communities. However, start where you can provide guidance, inside your company. Once your core team of Ethical Marketers is in place, they can take a closer look at how communication originates and is evaluated, as well as how ethical behavior plays out though your channels. Ethical Marketers find the problem areas. They can trace communication, from the planning phase and the creative and message development process to the channel selection and communication approvals, which should be complete with checks and balances. Add in the timing of distribution, measurement, and accountability, and you will start to see where potential faulty communication and undetected missteps can, or have, occurred.

There is an urgency for every business and their Ethical Marketers, participating in a dynamic media landscape, to place a greater emphasis on ethics. The journey begins by uncovering how stories, news and information are created and shared through different media channels, from broadcast and live streaming to online and social media.

In addition, stories no longer develop and get distributed solely through the communications department. They move across the organization and out to the public through any number of social channels, into your employees' professional and personal communities. For this reason, breaking down what is meant by ethics, values, and good judgment through your media channels is important. Then, you can educate others on the best practices going beyond the core team of Ethical Marketers. The practice should spread to rest of the company who is your army of ethical champions.

The Q&A included in this chapter focuses on businesses and their Ethical Marketers realizing how ethics may be challenged in digital marketing, social media and public relations programs. At the same time, all of the people within the organizations, who are excitedly sharing about their companies and the roles they play, need to embrace ethics and good judgment through their channels too. Applying ethics through your media channels is a practice the Ethical Marketers start and one that must be embraced by the entire collective body of ethical champions within the organization.

Q14 What are the big changes you have experienced with ethics in digital advertising?

Keeping up with the different ways that you can advertise today is one of the biggest challenges. You are constantly figuring out when and how to stand out in a very crowded landscape. The goal is to be heard, and to come across clearly and effectively in your communication. Whether your ads are nurturing a relationship, or they offer an audience a quick reason to engage, they are moving people from awareness to action and repeating the cycle frequently.

How do you do this in real-time without compromising your quality, integrity and credibility?

For the Ethical Marketer, real-time advertising creates "a get it done now" posture, which could also be seen as an "ask for forgiveness later" attitude. I have been mentored by leaders who have said that "80% done" is good enough and it is unrealistic to go for the 100% perfect. Of course, even at 80% you still want to have ethical guidelines, boundaries, and standards to practice. When you rush the process due to time pressures, marketers may find themselves leaving out important details, improvising or exaggerating, and compromising accuracy with human errors that could have been avoided.

I remember my agency was working on a campaign back in 2005, for a payroll company. We were on a tight deadline, but certainly not what would be considered today's real-time, social media deadline. One of our senior project managers was out that day and the ad traffic person was focused on several simultaneous client deliverables, with other campaigns she needed to get out of the door. One advertisement was a bit rushed, I guess you could say it was shy of the 80% mark, and we released it to the client. The client signed off quickly and the advertisement was sent to a trade publication for publication in hard copy format, as well as for the digital media campaign.

Of course, when the senior project manager returned to work the next day, she reviewed everything that left the marketing department in her absence. She saw a glaring mistake in the advertisement, which had already gone to print. It was a $60,000.00 mistake. We were not able to pull the first print advertisement. However, we did change the error in subsequent ads and the digital version was corrected immediately. Can you imagine? This was prior to the age of real-time advertising. Errors are human and forgivable. However, it was the lack of accountability, and not taking responsibility on our end, which was in very poor judgment. The senior leader in charge of the design team shifted blame to the client, who had signed off on an advertisement. As an agency and as an ethical partner, full accountability was necessary and, unfortunately, did not present itself immediately in this situation.

Even in the traditional sense there are errors and timing issues for marketers. So, how do you get those guardrails up when you want to respond with an ad during a real-time pop culture event? With more ethical guardrails in place, autonomy over process helps. For instance, the famous example of Oreo and "You Can Still Dunk in the Dark" during the Super Bowl XLVII. When the lights went out that year, as marketers would you want to wait? Instead, you want to seize the moment and push your advertisement or social media posts in a matter of minutes. When there are timing pressures and urgency to get your ad out, the number of mistakes may increase. The "normal" checks and balances are sometimes overlooked or reviewed quickly. However, Ethical Marketers figure out what expedited checks and balances look like and they become the standard.[3]

Ethical standards in advertising require marketers adhere to an objective truth and high standards when serving the public especially in real-time. Distinguishing these efforts becomes even more important when speed is of the essence.

Q15 When is an advertorial unethical?

Advertorials have long been regarded as the advertisements that do not resemble an ad. Marketers and PR professionals are creating messages, stories, images, and media, which appear as unbiased, helpful, and objective information. Yet, it is carefully devised messaging from the company, in the form of sponsored content or a native ad. Certainly, using advertorials is ethical. However, ethics are in question when your advertorial is not clearly seen as an advertisement framed in an editorial context.

Today, many consumers, but not all, are savvy about what they see and can identify what is strictly advertising versus a third-party credible endorsement (earned media) from the people they trust. However, in order to create a form of media that is helpful, and framed in a way that is also human, ethical, and pleasing to the eye, Ethical Marketers should adhere to these top tips for their advertorials:

- Make the clear distinction in the advertorial that your company is the sponsor of the advertorial or native advertising. Clearly represent that you are the business entity sharing the story or messaging displayed.
- Capture attention with genuine situations, actual customers and authentic viewpoints in your advertorial that make sense for your audience.

- Let your audience know your content is not earned media. Making content look like earned media is unethical.
- When you share advertorials on social media use distinguishing hashtags including #ad #sponsored #SponsoredAd and #sponsorship.

Because the lines are blurring between marketing, advertising and PR, and distinguishing types of campaigns is more difficult, it is even more important for customers to understand the difference between how they are being reached. You need to be clear in your marketing, so they don't mistake advertising and promotions for public relations and the earned media that is well-known for the trusted credible third-party endorsement.

Q16 What are false claims in marketing? Are they unethical or illegal?

Today, you hear and see all the disclaimers in pharmaceutical advertisements surrounding their products. For example, take the drug Dupixent, which is known to treat severe asthma. When you watch the Dupixent television commercial you receive information about the positive effects of the drug. However, at the end of the commercial, similar to any prescription drug product, you learn the long list of disclaimers about the negative side effects:[4]

- Do not use this product if you are allergic to Dupixent.
- Allergic reactions can occur including anaphylaxis, which is severe.
- Tell your doctor right away about signs of inflamed blood vessels, rash, shortness of breath, chest pain, or any tingling and numbness in your limbs.
- Do not take Dupixent if you have any parasitic infections.
- Stop any asthma medicines including oral steroids when using this product.

Despite all of the possible side effects and the "don'ts" for this drug, the advertisement still states, "You can du-more with less asthma," and to "Talk to your doctor about Dupixent." It would be unethical and illegal in terms of the product's advertising to omit any of the product disclaimers, regardless of the severity of the side effect.[5]

However, what about unsubstantiated claims you hear from celebrity doctors on TV who are sharing information about products. For example, Dr. Mehmet Cengiz Öz (known as Dr. Oz) was on Fox News offering his thoughts on a drug that was making big headlines in the news as a possible treatment for Coronavirus. During the segment, Dr. Oz shared his thoughts on the drug hydroxychloroquine, which is commonly used to treat malaria and lupus. Dr. Oz told Fox News host Sean Hannity that a French infectious disease specialist, who he spoke with previously, had said that using hydroxychloroquine and azithromycin may cause "trivial like rashes" which was the extent of the complications.[6]

After receiving backlash for his comments, Dr. Oz later took a more cautious stance toward hydroxychloroquine. The Veteran's Administration had also just released a study finding there was "no benefit" from the use of the drug in Covid-19 patients. At the same time, they discovered that more deaths occurred among the people who received the drug. Dr. Oz shifted his perspective in subsequent interviews.[7]

Ethical Marketers beware of what celebrities claim or what they share, whether it is under your guidance or even what they endorse on their own in interviews. Of course, if they are affiliated with your brand, then what they say can cause harm and can affect your reputation. Your good judgment is required. Be the conscious mind of the organization and be wary of what is fair, objective, and safe communication. People in challenging times look to the experts for their advice and guidance, not false and misleading claims.

Even if the influential personality is not officially representing your product, you have to be responsible to your consumers. Consider the comment made by President Trump about household cleaning products and Coronavirus, during his task force briefing, and how the media reported those comments. Clorox quickly rolled out with their clarifying statement. If there is any doubt as to how your customers will be influenced by what they see or hear from celebrities, politicians, or other influential individuals, then get your statements ready and distributed widely and quickly.[8]

False claims and misleading information, even when unintentional, are unethical, and in poor judgment. Brands cannot allow these types of comments to represent them and to confuse the public. They also cannot be "on the record" as factual information about their brands. It is up to you to err on the side of caution, especially when consumer safety is at stake. Follow the ethical rule here ... do no harm!

Q17 Do you have to be transparent in your digital advertising?

Yes, and you also have to consider how much transparency is enough transparency in your digital advertising. Full transparency is the best possible option when you are able to share all the information that is available to help people. Consumers want to make informed decisions on whether they will engage, experience, find out more information or purchase a product based on an advertisement. For this reason, brands creating and placing advertisements have to be transparent in appearance, use clear messaging and positioning of those ads, and deliver on their promises.

Consumers will judge companies and product ads based on their merits. They should be able to make informed decisions because the advertisement is truthful and accurate, the brand showcases what it values, and the brand is presenting all of the facts for an informed purchase. Brands who are tuned into their consumers know they care about transparency and feel empowered by the power of choice.

Here is a good example of transparency, stressing consumer choice. In May 2015, Panera Bread realized the importance of nutrition and choice in consumer food selection. They decided to revisit their menu and be much more transparent about each menu item, as well as animal rights and safety as they related to Panera's menu items. They rolled out with a campaign for their consumers which focused on a promise to avoid artificial ingredients. Full transparency required Panera to list all the nutritional elements for every food choice on their menu. They listed detailed ingredients, calorie intake per serving and nutrition facts. With this transparent campaign, Panera stressed healthy ingredients and supported consumer choice.[9]

For Panera, full transparency meant keeping an ongoing promise to avoid artificial ingredients and diving in deeper to provide those additional and detailed nutritional facts. Saying it in a campaign is one thing and showing it on your new menus is another. Panera let consumers know that full transparency was a part of their brand experience from the menu right to the table.

Q18 How can you avoid ethical issues with bloggers in your digital marketing?

Companies and their bloggers are equally responsible for ethics in digital marketing. If you are the company and you misinform your bloggers about the proper procedures and practices in your digital advertising or marketing programs, then you and your bloggers might pay an FTC fine. If your bloggers, on their own, are deceptive with marketing practices in your campaigns, then as the company working with them, you may also pay the price.

As an Ethical Marketer, you must know how to practice good judgment and carry the torch for the company to make sure all parties working with you are informed regarding good marketing and advertising practices. It is also the Ethical Marketer who is vocal about some of the blogging and marketing pitfalls to avoid. Be a more outspoken marketer by screening your bloggers carefully to see how they behave in other brand campaigns, and avoid the bloggers who do the following:

- Ask people for clicks to boost digital advertising; begging your audience to engage is not helping them to make an informed and authentic choice.
- Defame people by bullying or bashing people in public or in private, whether it is another public figure, influencer, or a customer, when they are on your payroll.

- Take a position of authority when is not their subject matter area of expertise.
- "Borrow" or claim content is theirs when it is, in fact, not theirs to share.
- Use improper digital advertising practices such as false clicks or "bot clicks" to boost their own advertising engine.
- Inflate their blogger status or social media numbers falsely to promote your product to an audience that does not necessarily need what you are offering.

It is extremely important for a company to know the blogger they are engaging. I was surprised to learn about an experiment by a business writer who pretended to be a candle "expert" and an influencer on Instagram. The writer of the magazine set up a fake Instagram account, bought 5,000 followers, stole photos from other Instagrammers, and used images that were not representative of her life. After making her account look authentic, as a true candle expert, she reached out to several candle manufacturers, who responded in kind. Two of the candle companies accepted her offer to be an influencer for their products. They based their decision on her social media profile, which was made up with photos that were not representative of her real brand.

Then, there were the two candle companies that declined her offer. The first one declined on the spot and the other one did a little digging into the writer's fake profile. They recognized the number of likes and comments on her profile did not match the engagement of an influencer with just over 5,000 followers. This candle company declined too.

To end the experiment, the writer decided to be transparent with the two companies that wanted to hire her and/or send free products. Only one, after learning the truth, was interviewed for her article. The other was angry at the fake profile and the reality of the situation.

In short, this is a perfect example of companies not doing enough homework to vet their bloggers and influencers. If bloggers and influencers are going to make unethical gestures, then it is up to Ethical Marketers to know what is real and what looks like a trouble spot for their companies.

Q19 Does GDPR affect ethics in your marketing programs and the content you share?

In April of 2016, Ethical Marketers were hearing about the General Data Protection Regulation (GDPR) in the European Union. The new regulation, which had to be fully implemented by May 2018, meant that companies marketing to consumers in the EU countries had to be mindful of new privacy and security protection measures. Companies in the EU, or even outside of the region marketing to these consumers within the region, were required to be more transparent in how they collected and used consumer data.

In other words, there was a new list of "dos" and "don'ts" for advertisers and marketers, which included:

- Making all data collection and storage policies public and easy for consumers to access.
- Having consumers "opt in" so that they understand and are in agreement with the ways you are collecting, using, and storing their data.
- Letting your customers decide how much data they are willing to share with you; offering an option such as this one builds trust.
- Deleting or erasing any customer data that are no longer being used.
- Being sure to have data collected and stored in a safe manner and allowing customers to update their privacy settings at any time.

Take Uber, for example. They have a good privacy policy that is not only easy to access, but also easy to digest. One of the larger issues with privacy policies is the length and fine print. All too often consumers will click the box just to move on to use a service. With the Uber policy you get the overview and highlights of key points. Uber also lets consumers know when their policies go into effect and the last date a policy was modified. They are also transparent by letting people see how data are collected and used.[10]

Whether it is a GDPR requirement or you are in the good practice of building trust with your consumers related to their data privacy and security, the more you can be transparent with them, the more you will grow and strengthen your relationship.

Q20 Who in your company is responsible for ethics in digital marketing?

There is an easy answer: the comprehensive team of Ethical Marketers, which goes up and down the communications line of command, right up to the CEO (the lead ethical role model), whether he or she signs off or not on the digital marketing. The comprehensive and collective body, or team researching, developing, executing, and measuring, is responsible for ethics from the start to the finish, and everything in between.

I remember when my agency was working with a non-profit associated with a high-profile Major League Baseball (MLB) player. We were developing the marketing collateral, PR programs and event production for the non-profit to help inner-city school children. Somewhere down the line there was a major break in communication and a signature of the MLB player was used in a piece of collateral, without sign off from his sports marketing agent.

Our agency was reprimanded quickly with a cease and desist letter and a number of steps were taken to rectify the poor judgment that was exercised. Immediately the fingers within the agency started pointing between the creative team who handled the marketing and advertising, and the PR team who was in charge of the media exposure for the non-profit's spokespeople, all the way up to the company partners. However, we were all on one team and we were going to rise together or fall together. Even though we took every action to fix the unethical missteps, we were sent the official notice that we were no longer the Agency of Record and we lost the account.

For our own learning and educational purposes, it was important to understand how our system broke down, and why and where we did not have the necessary checks and balances in place when producing a physical piece of content of such importance. We quickly realized we needed to update our guidelines and align with the proper protocols set by the sports agents and other marketing agencies we worked with. Whether it was the marketing or the PR team, it was THE collective team, so it did not matter. Everyone felt the sharp fall, including the company leaders, who lost an important relationship that had been cultivated over several years.

Whether you are servicing a client's brand, or it is your own in-house team, whoever has knowledge, and is a part of a communication process, ultimately has a responsibility to assure good judgment in decision-making through all of the designated communication channels.

When you can look beyond yourself to the collective whole, the entire team benefits from the conscience of the Ethical Marketers involved. The biggest lesson for the team is that you are not in this alone, so do not make choices alone.

Q21 Do digital marketers have to be concerned about privacy issues?

My mother was amazed at how quickly an advertisement popped up on Facebook after she visited a company's website. "How did they know?" I told her about Facebook Pixel and how you can retarget website visitors after they leave a company's site. Years ago, there was no Pixel advertising and when I was learning about PR and marketing, websites were not capturing and tracking consumer behavior. Today, digital marketers have a world of information at their fingertips. However, there is a trade-off for consumers; it is the customized information vs. the sharing personal information. Customers who want customized rely on Ethical Marketers.

Savvy consumers understand how everywhere you travel online you leave your digital footprint, whether you are just visiting a site or making a purchase from a favorite brand. You are being tracked too, and your data are quickly captured. There are privacy notices alerting consumers and they are more prominent today than ever before. However, are consumers really reading the policy statements? Do you? In some cases, they are not taking the time. For the companies who are actively spelling out how they collect information and use personal data, their customers are okay with these brands knowing so much about them, because of the personalized experience they receive. Yet, how much is too much information to give away? Clearly, there are consumers who would rather give their information away just for the ease and speed of getting what they need online, at any time of the day or night.

The decision by the consumer to share information is an important one for the Ethical Marketer to know and respect. However, if you want the rich information, then you have to be transparent and upfront about your efforts to collect and store data, which in and of itself has risks. Your customers may be okay with the collection and storing of their information. However, should a breach of their data occur, then what? This is a whole different story, for Ethical Marketers and their companies. Customers rely on you and trust that you will keep their data safe at all times and at all costs.

Data collection, storage and privacy are the responsibility of a business and their team of Ethical Marketers. The team has to educate openly, and with transparency, how the information is used and why this makes the experience better for a customer. Consumers are willing to share a great deal for a personalized experience. Regardless of how much or how little they share, your efforts must always reflect that of concern, interest, and care to maintain their trust by safeguarding privacy and keeping customer information secure at all times.

Of course, when the information is no longer safe, then it is also your responsibility to inform openly, with transparency, and to share the appropriate steps as to how you will do a better job to keep their data safe and maintain their future trust, if you still have the opportunity.

Q22 What is the best way to keep consumers informed about data privacy and security?

Consumers want privacy, yet they may not realize how much they are giving away when they share information. For Ethical Marketers it is not enough to have a little link at the bottom of your website that says "Privacy Policy" hoping your customers will find it and click on the link.

Companies, and their Ethical Marketers, are taking extra precautions by doing the following:

- Using language about "Cookies" that pops up immediately on websites alerting consumers that they are being tracked in an effort to optimize and personalize their experience.

- Educating consumers on what personal information is being collected and how it will be used and stored.
- Using website language, which consumers understand, and asking them to the accept terms regarding the collection and storage of their information.
- Updating consumers frequently on data privacy and being transparent with any new measures or changes to their data privacy and security policies.
- Limiting the amount of personal information collected; just because you can collect information does not mean you should collect ALL of it.
- Securing personal information with state-of-the-art encryption on your site.
- Encouraging conversations and questions about data privacy and security with consumers. Of course, if you are encouraging conversations then as an Ethical Marketer you should understand and be well-versed.
- Educating all employees in the company about consumer privacy; not just your team of Ethical Marketers, go beyond your marketing and PR departments.

What kind of safeguards do you have in place? How are you helping consumers to feel safe when they share information with you? Many of the practices you put in place may not be visible to your customers. Yet, the fact that you can take these precautions and let customers know how you are safeguarding their data makes a difference. Your business should be among the brands offering better experiences and also maintaining trust through their transparency.

Q23 Are there digital marketing practices that can get you banned from the search engines?

Have you heard the expression "gaming the system?" Unfortunately, every system can be "gamed" and search engines are no exception. Now, you may be saying, I'm not an SEO specialist, so why do I need to know? It goes back to the one collective ethical body and all parts of the system working together.

When it comes to search engines and being in good standing, here are some of the practices you want to avoid with your team:

- Posting duplicate content will get you penalized. However, if you are in a private community such as LinkedIn or Medium, you can repurpose blog content without fear of Google getting "annoyed."
- Having broken links on your site. If you don't keep your website free of pages not working and those annoying "404 Errors," then Google will let you know. Thus, your site ranking suffers.

- Using too many outbound links. There is a fine balance to offering additional linked resources. Also, be sure the links in your posts are active and they are not broken.
- Stuffing your content with keywords to be picked up in more consumer searches. The stuffing will get you penalized.
- Hiding links within your website is seen as unethical. All links should be visible and easily accessible for customers.
- Abusing the practice of link swapping with your website and promotional partners is frowned upon and seen as manipulating the search engines.
- Timing out, or the length of site down-time for extended periods, is not only inconvenient for consumers but you may also risk being de-indexed by a search engine.
- Buying paid links and having many different sites (especially the unrelated and irrelevant sites) point to yours can be seen as search engine manipulation.

JCPenney found out quickly that paid links can get you in trouble with Google and they can also create the appearance of search engine manipulation. Whether they were aware of what their search engine agency was doing or not, it still appeared that JCPenney was involved in a link scheme to increase its rankings. After the *New York Times* investigated JCPenney's search engine rankings and found an unusual number of unrelated sites pointing to their website, JCPenney fired their agency. JCPenney shared that it was not aware of the paid link program. Nonetheless, their missteps violated Google's guidelines and it was seen as unethical.[11]

Why not learn the latest in search engine best practices from the largest search engine, Google. Their Search Engine Optimization (SEO) Starter Guide is a good place to start.[12]

Q24 If you purchase a mailing list, then is it unethical if the people on the list have not "opted in" to receive information?

> "It's their fault!! We didn't do anything wrong ... the list company is the problem."

Okay, if you have said or heard this, then who vetted the list company? They did not do their own vetting. If you selected the partner company and you sent out the communication, then you are a part of the problem too. The people receiving the information you have shared through email won't say, "Oh, that darn list company!" On the contrary, they will be annoyed at the sender or the company's poor judgment for sending the unsolicited communication to them. At the same time, if consumers like what they receive from a company that has purchased from a list partner, they don't say, "Oh, I'm so glad a third-party shared my information." This is not the "normal" way of thinking.

What comes from the company is the responsibility of the company. Let me offer an example, although it does not pertain exactly to an email list company. Rather it is a company that gathers information about journalists, bloggers and media professionals in a database shared with PR professionals. PR pros can use the database to create customized media lists based on the information provided to share their news releases with these journalist and bloggers. Many journalists and bloggers in the database often wonder, "Why am I getting so many news releases and how did I get on this list." If your information is public then your credentials may end up in the system. As a blogger and podcaster myself, it is the reason I have the latest news, from many different businesses, flowing into my inbox every day.

The company's website clearly states that it has a database with more than 1.5 million contacts from traditional media to bloggers and social influencers. On occasion, I have received emails from the company to update my profile or to be removed from their system. There is also an opt-out option for any news release or pitch I receive that I no longer want.

Being on the receiving end of this information, I would say that seven out of 10 times, I am happy to receive the news, and the company sharing receives my praise. It is that "thank you company" for sending me this information rather than the "darn you, database company" for sharing my information in the first place. No matter what, the ethical approach behind the sharing still gives me a choice to opt-out.

When the purpose is good, the information is accurate and it comes from a place of helpful information, I'm all in and there is no reason to opt-out.

Q25 Are bloggers held to the same ethical standards as journalists?

Bloggers are not always held to the same journalistic standards as traditionally trained professionals who have studied journalism in college or postgraduate work. However, when writing for their communities, they still have to uphold values and good judgment, and be ethical in their communications.

I started blogging in 2007, and, wrapped in several hundred posts between then and now are facts, opinions, and my stream of consciousness on public relations, social media, technology, and the changes in the media landscape. I did not go to school for journalism, although I studied PR and communication and took a few journalism courses as a part my Bachelor of Arts degree. However, as I was creating my blog and gearing up for its launch, whether I had a journalism degree or not, wearing the badge of journalist did not cross my mind because bloggers were not journalists (even though the reverse is true … journalists can be bloggers).

My blog was all about my perspective and professional journey. Yes, like every human being, my views and how I see the world come with confirmation bias.[13] What shapes your personality and your world are accrued over years of learning and growth and it was the "flair" behind my blog writing.

However, having an opinion and sharing perspective is not without ethics. Having values and standards of conduct naturally came with the territory. If you are sharing professionally and offering advice and information, then this is not void of responsibility and accountability. Regardless of the format (maybe it is not AP journalistic style) you still have to be truthful, respectful, accurate in your examples and sources, and take a "do no harm" approach to any group when you are communicating.

Bloggers, like journalists, must take their ethics and values down every road they travel including where they share their written thoughts, opinions, and inspirations with their communities.

Q26 Is there a code of ethics for social media participation?

There is no single code of ethics for social media participation, whether you are a blogger and a citizen journalist sharing democratized content, or you work in-house at a company and you are an employee blogging as a part of a marketing/PR program. At least I could not find one. Yet, there are ways to access good resources to help you create your own set of standards.

Here are a few well-known resources for social media ethics to guide you:

- The PRSA Ethics and Social Media Advisory[14]
- Social Media Cases to Distill Ethical Guidelines by Dr. Shannon Bowen[15]
- The Arthur Page Society, Online Knowledge Center[16]

The resources shared are from professional PR associations and/or professionals in this area. However, any number of industry associations are building and constantly refining their own social media ethics for members in their field. From the National Library Association to the medical and science communities and technology, professionals turn to their industry organizations for knowledge and best practices.

Companies also have a responsibility to provide their employees with social media guidelines that include ethical communication practices. Within a social media policy, employees learn good judgment as they engage professionally and personally in their social media communities. For example, good judgment may include:

- **Writing responsibly.** Being accurate and honest to build integrity with community members.
- **Being authentic.** Delivering information transparently, identifying yourself and your role in our company.

- **Considering your audience.** Being mindful that readers of your posts include current and potential clients.
- **Avoiding fights.** Steering away from unnecessary or unproductive arguments and inflammatory/objectionable topics.
- **Understanding the concept of community.** Realizing that online communities exist so you can support others.

However, ethical responsibility also extends to all members of the company's community. Organizations will also create social media guidelines weaving their values and ethics in their public facing social media policies too. These guidelines let all community members know the acceptable behaviors and frame out how good social media citizens participate by sharing, learning, and growing together.

Here is an example of standard outward-facing and helpful social media public guidance to keep all social media citizens engaged and sharing in a productive way. Organizations will educate community members on participation that avoids:

- Violating any laws, whether they are local, state, or international, including copyright and intellectual property rights laws.
- Sharing content or material that is unlawful, disruptive, threatening, profane, obscene, defamatory, abusive, intimidating, or offensive.
- Posting advertisements, solicitations, or "spam" of any kind.
- Impersonating any person or entity or falsely stating or misrepresenting your relationship with a person or entity.
- Transmitting any material that infringes upon a patent, trademark, trade secret, or other proprietary rights of any party.

The company's Ethical Marketers are also the "community police" in their online communities, letting all social media participants know that activities are monitored, and they can prohibit, restrict or block access to any of social media properties at their sole discretion.

Being socially responsible and good social media citizens is not just for a company's employees; it is for all parties who actively participate in the social media community engagement.

Q27 How can you spot a bot on social media to avoid sharing misinformation?

There are a number of ways to recognize a bot and to distance yourself from misinformation. However, bots are getting more sophisticated and they are not as easily detected today. Before spelling out what to identify, first let's discuss the nature of the bot and which bots are harmful.

According to Wikipedia, a bot, which is the simplified term for web robot or robot, is a software application that can perform repetitive, simple tasks. These tasks can be done so much more quickly than a human. If you think about accomplishing actions or functions at an expedited rate, then you can see there would be some useful functions for bots. For example, bots are helpful when they are being used as virtual assistants and they can easily personalize information for your customers. Bots are helpful when they are answering detailed questions with respect to customer service inquiries or product information requests. They can be used when scheduling appointments from your doctor's visit to your next car service appointment. Not every bot is a bad actor.

However, like all technology, there is the functional and useful, and then there is the less than desirable and even harmful. When it comes to sharing news and information on social media, "Houston we have got a problem" and it is a bot problem. In 2019, the Institute of Engineering and Technology reported that bots are becoming more difficult to detect and they are "designed to influence the trajectory of discourse on social media ..."[17] As a matter of fact, out of 250,000 active users discussing both the 2016 Presidential election and the interim 2018 election, approximately 30,000 were bots. What is even more concerning is how bots are able to successfully imitate what looks like legitimate human engagement.

For this reason, here is what Ethical Marketers need to keep on their radar to spot the inauthentic bot. Take a good look at their social media profiles and their participation habits. Bots are known to:

- Have avatars that are not symmetrical. For example, you may see an image of a woman wearing different earrings in her ears, or a man who has two different size ears. The photo is a "tell" that you are interacting with a bot.
- Retweet information at a very fast pace. Bots are also known to retweet a bunch of people who are sharing the same type of information.
- Use language that is algorithmic and not human-like. You can tell by the way their posts are almost formulaic and repetitive.
- Follow fewer humans yet they follow more bots. If you take a look at the suspected bot's followers, then you will see more of the same bot-like characteristics.
- Miss the meaning behind a conversation and often change the subject; humor completely goes over a bot's "head."

If Ethical Marketers can be role models to spot the bots and stop the sharing of what's fake and misleading, then this is a good step toward decreasing the misinformation or the disinformation that is propagated in social media communities.[18]

Q28 Who in your company is responsible for ethics in social media?

You might think the answer to the "who is responsible for social media ethics" is similar to who is responsible for digital marketing. It is, and it is not, at the same time. So, yes, the responsibility does fall on your team of Ethical Marketers in your communications department. It is this team that is involved in the social media campaign and who are directly responsible from the creative conception to proper execution, measurement and accountability. So, yes, the professionals who work, monitor closely, engage in social conversations, and measure/report the outcome up the chain of command, are responsible.

Yet, social media takes a different communication structure. What starts as owned media out of the company quickly becomes shared by other members of your company and the public. As soon as communication leaves the communication department there is good news and there are precautions. The good news is that having any of your champions, including employee champions from various departments, share your social media communications is great for your brand. There is nothing better than your own people being passionate and proud of their company. At the same time, the bad news is you are no longer steering the ethical ship, and missteps and poor judgment can surface quickly.

Companies are excited to watch social media programs become recognized and embraced with internal employee champions, customer ambassadors and the public at large. Realizing and sharing the responsibility for ethics across the organization is a big reason why the excitement and positive momentum grows. At the same time, keep those Ethical Marketers closely connected (especially the PR people) to the online conversations, should the pendulum swing in the other direction toward unwanted and issue-related communications.

Q29 Is buying followers on social media an unethical practice?

Social media is about authenticity. Early on, businesses realized that open and transparent communication was the best approach to social media communications. Your community members want to know the real "you," whether it is your personal brand or the professionals behind the four walls of your company. People participating in social communities expect a certain level of transparency and through this transparency you can build trust in your relationships.

Purchasing followers is not showing how you want to build trust and it is not revealing your true authentic self on social media. You have to ask yourself, what do you value ... real relationships or fake impressive-looking numbers? When you buy your followers, you are actually sending a signal to your community that it is more important to focus on the numbers than it is to build real organic social media relationships.

Many professionals on social media do not realize how buying followers demonstrates poor judgment and is also easily spotted by your community members. The trained social media community member knows the signs of purchased followers, which are:

- The profile numbers are close in count. Most organic growth shows that you follow fewer people than who actually follow you.
- When you analyze a profile's followers using a social media tool, you are able to see a large spike during a particular timeframe on or about the purchase date of followers.
- A large percentage of the influencer's followers are not industry professionals or people who would be of interested in this person's expertise.
- The quality of the comments on the influencer's profile look spammy and are not adding any value to the conversation.
- The influencer's followers have very little or no information on their profiles.

These are all signs or the first red flags when you are looking at the numbers. Bear in mind, it is not the numbers that make the influencers, it is the relationships. Authenticity of your brand, which shows in your followers too, is the first indication and it also reveals what you value.

Q30 What should you do if you make an unethical misstep on social media?

Missteps happen all the time. It is what you do after the misstep that counts the most. When you make a mistake, it is better to own up to it, correct the record, be accountable and yes, apologize if that is what your customers or constituents would expect from you.

You may be wondering ... then how do so many people get away with sharing misinformation and doubling down without an apology? Please keep in mind the nature of your brand. Yes, it is always what people expect from you. A brand that is built on trust, reliability, sound advice, truth and accuracy should not avoid making the inevitable apology. Make it quickly to mitigate any reputational damage.

On the contrary, what about the brand that is full of "vim and vigor," a confrontational fighter and a brand that has a "take no prisoners" attitude? Well, this is a brand that people may not look to for an apology, and/or would not expect one. Cognitive dissonance would occur if this brand changed its course and was inconsistent with its behavior. Whether it is right, wrong or there is indifference, brands live up to what is expected by their loyal fans. The brand champions become the people who dictate the brand approach, and there will be repercussions if the delivery of information does not meet their expectations.

For example, there are politicians who will explain what President Trump meant when he makes a statement on Twitter, which some groups deem harmful. No one is expecting an apology or reversal from the President. Watching his administration explain, or his loyal advocates sharing what he meant, is also representative of their brands. It does not matter how alarming the tweets sound, but rather how "on point" it might seem to the millions of people who are following the President with enthusiasm. In this case, regardless of the ethics discussion, there is no expectation for President Trump to apologize in the minds of his loyal followers. Perhaps, for his critics, there is hope that one day he will. However, hope is not a brand strategy that the media, the critics, or the opponents of the President can rely on during this presidency.

If you make an unethical misstep and share something that is misinformation, then as an Ethical Marketer, think about what people would expect from you, understanding how they rely on you. When you answer this question, then it will guide the nature of the apology; when, where and how it is delivered.

For me, an apology has a few parts to keep in mind:

- The words, "I'm sorry for ...," which is better than the more formal words "I apologize," or "We apologize for ..." The tone and the intent of an apology go a long way.
- The delivery of your apology matters right down the channel. Do you have to get on camera and show that you are sorry with a video apology? Now, it is not just your words and intent, it is also showing through your body language that you are truly sorry.
- Go beyond your words into action steps. The steps you take to render the situation and make it right for the people who count on you is what matters the most. It is not just the "I'm sorry for what has happened." Instead, it is the careful process the Ethical Marketer puts into place to prevent a similar occurrence from ever happening again.

At the same time, those values that you have carved out for yourself (in Chapter 1, Learning the Essentials), aligned with your organization, will also help to guide you toward the best approach to handling any missteps and a subsequent apology.[19]

Whatever you do, consider the ethics, and also be true to your brand.

Q31 Is it ethical to hide or delete posts on social media, if you know that the information may be damaging to your brand?

Is hiding anything ever a good answer? When it comes to hiding or deleting posts you have to determine whether the post comes in the form of helpful critique, negative criticism or harmful words and hurtful action.

The minute you open up your social media channels, you are giving the public a "green light" to share their opinions with you, which can come in the form of helpful criticism or harsh critique. When people take the time to show up and voice a concern, it shows they care. Not all negative criticism comes from a place of hurt. You have to determine the nature of the comment and where it is coming from.

Of course, there is no room for hurtful and harmful. Companies can and should delete social media posts presented as abusive, defamatory and harmful language. However, when you come across a concern, negative feedback or harsh criticism, whether it is directed at your personal or professional brand, or it is directed at your company, investigate the comment and address it as quickly as you can. Hiding or deleting a post from a concerned customer or someone who has a strong opinion will lead to a floodgate of more negative or harsh opinions.

Early on, I learned how transparency is rewarded in social media communities. You can make an inadvertent misstep and the critics will appear. However, when you address issues with understanding and care, you can change the situation. At the same time, an authentic brand will and should have comments that are not always glowingly positive. No one and no brand are perfect. I am yet to see the social media newsfeed or profile wall that has all positive comments. Perhaps, they are out there. However, the world we live in is rich in perspective and with different perspectives comes all sides of a critique or the gift of feedback. You should not ward off or fight what is actually a gift. Regardless, if the gift appears negative, you can still embrace it and move a relationship forward onto much better footing.

Get rid of the harmful and the rest is your choice. However, what is authentic and actually human cannot be perfect on social media.

Q32 What should you do if you are being trolled by someone who is acting unethically?

Just the word "trolled" alone tells you how to approach this situation ... with caution. I had an experience with a troll during a client's public Twitter chat. My client was one of the special guests, on a panel of experts, participating in a popular influencer's tweetchat discussion. My PR team counseled the client beforehand, reminding him to focus on the tweets from specific handles, including the moderator and the other panelists. We also instructed him to be on the lookout for our tweets, as we would be retweeting and tagging him in any additional questions and conversations to guide his participation. We mentioned he should stay away from conversations and handles that were not participating in the good spirit of the chat session, and who may also "look like trolls" acting suspect, using defamatory language and demonstrating poor judgment.

Well, the instructions were easier said than done. A troll entered the tweetchat with a legitimate and unintimidating question that appeared valid to my client and then the conversation quickly went downhill from there. As soon as the troll engaged our client, along came five more trolls jumping into the discussion. Also present in the stream of tweets came the profanity, the name calling, and the very, very bad behavior. Yes, poor judgment, to say the least, was obvious, and the Standard Operating Procedure (SOP) for Ethical Marketers is to avoid the trolls and not engage with them. However, you or the PR team should always monitor them closely. Seeing our client engage and break protocol reminded me of a situation you witness in an action movie where you see a military commander yelling, "Abort the mission, go back, do not proceed!" except this situation was playing out on social media.

The rule here is to let the trolls be the ones who exhibit the bad behavior and the poor judgment. At some point, the moderator of the Twitter chat shared a tweet reminding everyone "this is an educational Twitter chat meant to help students and professionals," reinforcing the mission of the community and the focus of the tweetchat participants. Eventually, as the uplifting and educational information continued to flow, and the trolls were completely ignored, they went away to harass another community and expert.

You cannot change the values of the trolls who join your discussion. You cannot make them behave ethically. However, as an Ethical Marketer, you can make a choice not to go down the wrong path with them. When it comes to trolls and your good judgment, always take the high road.

Q33 Do you have to engage with everyone on social media, especially if you're not in alignment with their values?

If you went to a friend's party and you saw a group of guests acting in ways that did not sit well with you, then would you want to hang out with these guests all night? Perhaps they were spilling drinks on the host's carpet, roughhousing and breaking glasses in her living room, placing their feet on the furniture and exhibiting behavior you wouldn't tolerate in your own home.

If your answer is no, absolutely not, then it is most likely because you do not identify with their values or their behavior. Your values do not align with theirs. You expect your friends to be respectful and to take care in someone's home, as if it were their own. Why, then, do so many people friend, follow, like, share and tolerate behavior on social media they don't find acceptable? What is the difference?

There is no difference. You have the same choice on social media. At the start of the interaction, it is your choice. The onus is on you to observe behavior and know who it is you are about to engage. From the looks of a potential "friend's" profile to reviewing past conversations, there are tell-tale signs of how they will participate on social media with you.

Of course, at any time in a relationship, whether it's a new friend or someone who has been a part of your community, you can make the decision to unfollow if they are acting in ways that challenge your values. Being aligned and feeling like there is a mutual benefit is an important part of your social relationships and your brand's experience.

When you compromise the value of your connections, you reap what you sow. The result is noise, confusion, and behavior that does not align with your own.

Q34 How do you report unethical behavior on social media?

First, you have to give people a way to report unethical behavior on different social media platforms. Ethical Marketers should make it easier for employees within the company to reach out through designated channels with their concerns about other members of the organization, as well as any company stakeholders who are participating, without fear of repercussions. At the same time, every employee has a responsibility to act with respect, responsibility, and to be the unofficial representative of their company. Even beyond a company's social properties, an employee's company title is recognized by the public as an extension of the company brand.

Recognizing bad behavior also means teaching what good judgment is and what it is not. Companies have been creating and changing their social media policies and guidelines, so employees know the difference between helpful and valuable participation and unacceptable conduct.

Companies like Walgreens, IBM, Walmart and Ford Motors go to great lengths to build their social media playbooks and social media policies. When I was working with a digital marketing agency, their social media playbook and social media policy was an integral part of their brand. The founder of the firm believed in "Learning for Life" and these social media resources were a testament to ongoing learning as technology and the media landscape continued to evolve. The days of a static policy and set of guidelines were over. With respect to this agency, their social media playbook came complete with an incentive program to get employees excited about participating and created healthy competition among different departments and teams in the company.

Social media playbooks are set in place as a preventative measure. The more you invest in the development and creation of these resources, the more your employees will be your champions to create opportunities on social media and to spot what you need to know that might be harmful for your brand.

Once again, prevention through a playbook cuts back on having to report the "abuse."

Q35 What is "fake news" and how does it challenge your ethics?

One of the issues with fake news is actually discerning whether it is fake or not. Unfortunately, the term "fake news" runs rampant in our social media communities as much as the media and news platforms have committed to investigating harmful fake news.

Is there a way to spot fake news? Yes, with patience, your careful eye, critical thinking, your instincts, and good judgment. Ethical Marketers, it is time to apply your professional skill set to identify what is good, sourced news deserving of attention and sharing, and what is a part of the "propaganda machine" created as misinformation and funneled into your own echo chamber on social media.

Remember, every marketer is a consumer, with preconceived notions and perceived bias that shapes viewpoints, so let the buyer beware. Wherever you receive your news on social media, remember that you are being served information that aligns with your preferences and what you have been viewing previously. The social media algorithms on Facebook, Instagram and other communities serve up what you like and expect, and give you more of the same.

You can take your blinders off by remembering the following:

- **Haste Makes Waste.** When it comes to US politics, the lesson here is: Do not be in too much of a hurry to share what you see or read on social media. There is a greater need to fact check as news cycles are 24/7 and they quickly turn out misstatements and misinformation in high volumes, from politicians and government entities. Two examples of good fact-checking sources are FactCheck.org and Politifact.com.
- **The Publisher Matters.** In order to stop the sharing of misinformation, Ethical Marketers have to take it upon themselves to research the publisher and explore the background of the media outlet. Is it a reputable publication with credentials? If it is a blogger, who is this person and what are this person's background and credentials? One way to vet is to determine whether the news articles would meet an academic standard, which is more descriptive, analytical, critical, and thorough.
- **A URL Says A Lot.** You can spot fake news by evaluating the news article link. For example, abcnews.com is okay. However, be wary of

abcnews.com.co or any news site with a .com.co. Wikipedia has a fake news page where you will see several examples of .com.co fake sites.[20]

- **Reverse the Search.** Not only can you reverse search the source of an article, but you can also reverse search an image too. All too often, with the ability to Photoshop, it has become easier to alter images. A reverse search helps you to uncover the origins of news article or image, which includes the original source and approximate first date of publishing.[21]
- **Quotes & More.** You can spot fake news by the lack of expert quotes and outside sources used within the article or blog post. This is a tell-tale sign that the news is not meeting journalistic standards, especially when you see several prominent voices, mentioned by name and title, being quoted as credible experts by other news outlets.

Q36 How do you communicate ethically if you accidentally share or breach confidential information?

I remember working with a social media data intelligence company who experienced a data breach of their customers' information. The IT team was the first to recognize a breach had occurred. They followed the standard protocol in a "crisis" situation to alert the executive team who then alerted the lawyers. The PR team was briefed so they could begin drafting statements for the company's customers, the media and analysts, their employees and the groups who needed to know what had happened.

The first consideration when you accidentally share, or there is a breach of, confidential information, is to figure out who needs to hear from you first. You should tell the truth, sharing your story quickly before anyone else shares this story for you. We asked, "Who needs to know what, and when are we able to share?" We did not ask, "What should we say that will help the company to make us look better?" It is at this juncture that your values come into play.

Customers were the first to know and learn about the situation. When your customers' data are compromised, if you do not share what happened, and how you are going to make the situation better, with your action steps to prevent a future breach, then you compromise and/or lose their trust. Getting to the customers first, so they can hear from you, is paramount. Ethical Marketers know that customers should not hear about a data breach from their favorite business publication or from members of their social media communities.

Of course, you have to share with your employees too. Employees, especially those who interface directly with customers as a part of their roles, need a statement, updated information on the situation, and where they can direct customers, and other interested parties, to the people who can answer their questions.

At the same time, a big mistake companies make, depending on the scope of the breach and the subsequent news, is not informing the employee population about what to do if they receive inquiries or if they are faced with questions on social media. They, too, should have information, whether it is an area of the company's website where questions are answered or where updates are posted. If it is not a part of their official role, then these employees should not field customer questions or media inquiries. Knowing who in the company can answer these questions is crucial.

Then, there is the media who will want to know what has happened and how many customers were affected. If the media comes knocking, then this is an opportunity to provide updates and accurate information rather than leaving the media to report your story or have the story reported by the business pundits in your industry. For the media, you should be prepared with the timing of the situation, what you know to date (that can be shared), how you are handling the situation, and what you are doing to ensure the security of customer data from that point onward. Also be prepared for the questions you do not want them to ask and how you will handle these types of difficult questions.

From an ethical perspective, you want to be transparent, considerate of the timing, and take accountability for the breach. Trying to blame your customers by saying, "customers should know there are risks involved when they enter their personal information online or when they want to use our service" will not help your brand. You will not build back the trust. Quite the opposite; it leads to customers taking their business elsewhere.

Do breaches happen? Yes, they do. Can you always prevent them? Probably not, as hackers become increasingly more sophisticated. However, you can be open, honest, and be a partner who shows integrity and character by caring and understanding the severity of the damage. You can offer communication to let your customers and the market know you are not only in "control" of the situation, but also you are taking every measure to place your best foot forward.

Q37 If you are measuring PR program results based on older PR measurement values, is this considered unethical?

Using outdated measurement is unethical as a partner who should be advising clients that there are more effective ways to measure. For example, there is an ongoing debate over Advertising Value Equivalents (AVEs) being used as a viable PR measurement practice. Clients have asked me to track AVEs, and I have declined by offering them a better measurement solution. Your client may not think it is unethical, however, it is not in their best interest and misleading for their business.

Whether it is the type of measurement, the accuracy and the accepted standard, companies base their decisions on the numbers. The data you collect are a driver to shaping future communications programs. When my agency was working with a telecommunications firm, we knew AVEs were not an acceptable form of measurement; they were misleading. The client wanted to use AVEs because it was easy to track as they were using trade publications for both advertising and editorial placements. We, however, were moving beyond the trades and also into business publications as part of a larger growing industry trend. Rather than just adhering to a faulty standard of measurement we pressed for different measurement benchmarks that helped leaders to see the value of the public relations work and the stories being generated.

Although more difficult to score and measure, we were looking at how the messaging was resonating with the journalists and how this related to public opinion. We tracked messaging to see how often the client was mentioned as a part of the media coverage and then a larger social media conversation. We also were looking at clear ways to track customer engagement, from the time they read a news story to their behavior once they landed at the company's website. As a true partner, it was in everyone's best interest to try a new measurement approach.

The ethical challenge lies in the people and the partnership. At times, the higher numbers are what secures the account and the PR work. AVEs can show big numbers and other forms of tracking do not. However, the Ethical Marketer would rather build the momentum with a new set of numbers and a solid measurement that shows traction, rather than an outdated approach with very little value. Ethical Marketers see past the large number that appears impressive and find the path to what is the real value.

The Marketing Experts "Weigh In" on Ethical Guidance

Remember Who You Are and What You Stand For

By Gini Dietrich, founder of Spin Sucks and CEO, Arment Dietrich

When we were teenagers and were heading out on the town for the night, my mom would say to every one of us, "Remember who you are and what you stand for." At the time, we all rolled our eyes at her, not even completely understanding what she meant. But when friends were drinking and smoking pot (or worse), we remembered who we were and that we were taught those things were bad for us (and irresponsible for teenagers). Not to say we didn't get into any trouble, especially my brothers, but it was a good mantra to live by.

It's a mantra that has followed me into adulthood and my professional life, too. If you think about how that fits your online use, it works perfectly. Who are you? What do you stand for? What are your values and your morals? How do you feel when someone does something you don't want to participate in? How do you expect others to treat you? How do you treat others?

The answers to these questions are both existential and can guide the ethics across your media channels. If your guiding principle for how you participate online is always ethics first, it won't matter what changes are made to the social networks, what changes are made to the Google algorithm, or what crisis has last hit the world. That's not to say you won't make mistakes. You will. But when you are ethical above all else—both online and off—you'll quickly recover. Own up to the mistake, apologize, and move on.

At the same time, the ethical way you approach your communications allows you to be inclusive and it allows you to be aware of others' perspectives and opinions. While one of the most challenging things for human beings is to be open to what others think and how they behave, it creates social well-being for your business and your business relationships.

This means you should be aware, always, of who can see your information, what you share, and what is being said and shared about your organization. Overall, your online presence should create a positive, credible perception for your benefit—and for that of your customers, your stakeholders, your employees, your ambassadors, and even your critics.

My grandfather is a Facebook friend and I always think, "Will I be mortified if Grandpa sees this?" You can ask yourself the same question, "Would my grandparents (or parents) approve of this?" If it passes the grandma test, it's typically OK to post.

Ethics are very personal. What works for you might not work for others and vice versa. So, I will leave you with the advice from my mom: remember who you are and what you stand for. If you do that, what you post online will always stand the test of time.

Applying Ethics Through Your Media Channels

By Martin Waxman, President, Martin Waxman Communications

In late Summer 2001, I was working for an independent PR agency in Toronto. And our biggest client, a major manufacturer of consumer goods, was about to launch a travel pack for one of its products.

Now, this wasn't a stop the presses type of innovation by any means. It was simply a brand extension. And anyone familiar with consumer PR would know the news value of most brand extensions is minimal at best. (Except on a slow news day—remember those?)

In any event, we came up with what we thought was a creative way to at least get a modicum of media attention. We purchased a bunch of those silver metal lunchboxes that resembled old luggage. On the front, we attached stickers of London, Paris, and New York. Inside, we placed the product, a bottle of water, an apple and the media materials folded inside an 8" x 4" mailer designed to look like a boarding pass.

We distributed it to media by overnight courier on September 10.

And then 9/11 happened ...

On September 12, we started getting calls from news outlets saying they received our metal package and didn't care what was in it, their security team informed them we had to pick it up right away.

Our Ethical Dilemma

After the second call. I knew there was little chance we could salvage the idea or get coverage for it, not in a few days or weeks—possibly not ever. What started as a cute and somewhat innocuous plan had suddenly turned offensive. And it was our responsibility to figure out what the best course of action would be, inform our client, and take it from there.

I believed then—and still do today—that we needed to be completely open and up-front with the client. So, I called her, explained the situation and said we had to put this program on hold. I also told her we would monitor the landscape and keep her updated on how we might be able to proceed but couldn't offer anything more concrete than that.

The client heard us and pushed back, asking us to develop an out of the box way to start pitching this in a week. We listened but held our ground, reiterating our concerns. and eventually she did come around.

Ultimately, our client realized that in extraordinary situations—including pretty much any major crisis—business as usual no longer applies. When this happens, promotions need to stop immediately because there are bigger and more pressing issues to deal with. And while much has changed since then—especially with regards to the media and channels we use—that lesson shaped the way I approach communications during a crisis situation to this day.

If a tragedy occurs and an organization asks me what's the right thing to do, I tell them to put all promotional activities on hold, assess the situation and its impact, and then wait, watch, analyze and adapt.

What is Truth?

By Dick Martin, Author, former Executive VP of Public Relations, AT&T

What, after all, is truth?

Philosophers have been arguing about the meaning of "truth" for millennia. A barebones, dictionary definition of truth is "conformity to facts." But we now live in a time of "alternative facts." The late Senator Daniel Patrick Moynihan once said that people are entitled to their own opinions, but not to their own facts. Behavioral science suggests his analysis was, at best, aspirational.

Few of us consider the facts before forming an opinion. We are all more likely to filter available facts through our pre-existing opinions. It happens unconsciously, driven by ancient mental gymnastics—like confirmation bias and selective hearing—that were more suited to protecting us from dangers in the jungle than navigating modern society. To help counter those distortions, over the years, I've developed a working definition of truth in the practice of public relations.

Truth is all the information a reasonable person needs to make an intelligent, voluntary decision, free of coercion.

That's the level of truth people should have before deciding to buy a company's products, work for it, invest in it, or welcome it into their community. It reflects a deeper understanding of PR's role in the construction of meaning.

Think about it: isn't that what PR is all about? Whether informing, persuading, or mediating, we're working with people's current feelings, attitudes, and understanding to construct a new meaning for our company, organization, or brand. Ideally, a meaning favorable to our client.

But meaning exists across a continuum, from meaningless to meaningful. And from misleading to truthful. Ethical PR operates at the meaningful and truthful end of that continuum.

It can answer "yes" to these five questions:

- Is what I'm doing or saying grounded in **good purpose**? That is, does it give people all the information they reasonably need to make an intelligent decision?
- Does it **respect** people's human dignity and right to reason? That is, am I treating people as means to what I want or as individuals who have goals of their own? Am I manipulating their emotions or reasoning to the point that they're incapable of making a truly voluntary decision?
- Does it demonstrate **care** for their well-being? Would I consider it good if I were in their position?
- Is it in the larger **public interest**? Do my goals serve the general welfare of society? Am I violating anyone's rights? Am I respecting the foundational principles of free societies, such as a free press and the right to assembly?
- Can I be **proud** of what I'm doing or saying? Would my parents, spouse, or kids say it reflects the kind of person I claim to be?

While these questions may sound theoretical, they have practical application. For example, I was once asked if it was acceptable to follow a widely accepted custom in some foreign countries of giving reporters an envelope of cash to encourage them to write favorably about the company.

It really was common in that country at the time. Reporters expected it. All our competitors did it. And the cost of not doing it was clear—ranging from no coverage to negative coverage.

Some told me it was no different than tipping a waiter. Reporters, like waiters, work for low wages; they depend spin tips to get by. And who are we to challenge local customs?

But it seemed to me that paying reporters to run a news release violates a number of ethical principles.

- Paying for a good story is not a legitimately **"good purpose."** When people read a newspaper, they expect articles free from outside influences. Even on the assumption the release contained no misleading information, its appearance in the paper would give it news value it might not otherwise have, which is, in itself, misleading.
- Hiding the payment doesn't **respect** readers' rights to reason by depriving them of information that would almost certainly influence their opinion of the resulting story.
- Rather than demonstrating **care** for the reporter's readers, our potential customers, it harms them by violating their right to full information, including the fact that the story was a paid placement.
- Paying for the news to be run, without revealing it, is not in the **public interest.** It corrupts one of any democracy's key institutions—a free press.
- No one could be **proud** of this practice. It's clearly dishonest; otherwise, why the envelope? Tipping a waiter is done in the open for everyone, including the waiter's employer, to see. But the waiter's employer would likely frown on a gratuity quietly slipped to a server prior to the meal to ensure priority service. Such behavior would put other diners at a disadvantage and endanger the employer's reputation.

Answer those five questions and you will be tapping into the major theories of ethical decision making over the last 2,500 years. Fail to answer "yes" to any, and you'll just confirm what most people already think of public relations practitioners.

Notes

1 Deirdre Breakenridge, "PR Practice #7: Reputation Task Force Member Chart of Responsibilities," PR Strategies Blog, https://www.deirdrebreakenridge.com/pr-practice-7-reputation-task-force-member-chart-of-responsibilities, June 2012.
2 Gini Dietrich, "What is the PESO Model?" Spin Sucks Blog, https://spinsucks.com/communication/peso-model-breakdown, September 2020.
3 Staff Writer, "2013: Oreo wins the Superbowl with 'dunk in the dark' tweet," The Drum, https://www.thedrum.com/news/2016/07/10/marketing-moment-101-oreo-wins-super-bowl-dunk-dark-tweet, March 2016.

4 Dupixent Website, https://www.dupixent.com/atopicdermatitis/dupixent-resour ces/frequently-asked-questions, September 2020.
5 iSpotTV, Dupixent TV Commercial, Du-More with Less Asthma, https://www. ispot.tv/ad/o9mr/dupixent-du-more, 2019.
6 Melanie Arter, "Dr. Oz: Complications from Hydroxychloroquine Were 'Trivial Like Rashes.'" CNSNews, https://www.cnsnews.com/article/national/melanie-a rter/dr-oz-complications-hydroxychloroquine-were-trivial-rashes, April 2020.
7 Ted Johnson, "Dr. Oz Now Says of COVID-19 Treatment Hydroxy-chloroquine: 'We are Better Off Waiting,'" https://deadline.com/2020/04/dr-oz-now-says-of-covid-19-treatment-hydroxychloroquine-we-are-better-off-waiting-1 202914838, April 2020.
8 Diana Bradley, "Lysol and Clorox respond to Trump comment about injecting disinfectant," PRWeek, https://www.prweek.com/article/1681380/lysol-clorox-re spond-trump-comment-injecting-disinfectant, April 2020.
9 Alida, "Five Brands That Employed Transparency in Marketing and Won," http s://www.alida.com/the-alida-journal/5-brands-employed-transparency-marketing -and-won, July 2016.
10 Greer Williams, "GDPR: 5 Examples of Well-Presented Privacy Policies," Pact-safe, https://www.pactsafe.com/blog/gdpr-5-examples-of-well-presented-priva cy-policies, August 2018.
11 Vanessa Fox, "New York Times Exposes J.C. Penney Link Scheme That Causes Plummeting Rankings in Google," Search Engine Land, https://searchenginela nd.com/new-york-times-exposes-j-c-penney-link-scheme-that-causes-plummeting -rankings-in-google-64529, February 2011.
12 Google Help Center, General Guidelines, Search Engine Optimization Starter Guide, https://support.google.com/webmasters/answer/7451184?hl=en, September 2020.
13 Iqra Noor, "Confirmation Bias," Simply Psychology, https://www.simplyp sychology.org/confirmation-bias.html, June 2020.
14 Ethics and Social Media PDF, Public Relations Society of America (PRSA) website, https://www.prsa.org/docs/default-source/about/ethics/eas/ethical-sta ndards-advisory-ethics-and-social-media.pdf?sfvrsn=be47b4cb_2, September 2015.
15 Dr. Shannon Bowen, "Ethics in an Age of PR and Social Media Conversations," PR Strategies Blog, https://www.deirdrebreakenridge.com/ethics-in-an-age-of-so cial-media-public-conversations, July 2013.
16 Arthur Page Society, "The Dynamics of Public Trust in Business," Online Knowledge Base, https://knowledge.page.org/report/the-dynamics-of-public-trus t-in-business-emerging-opportunities-for-leaders, September 2020.
17 E&T Editorial Staff, "Social media bots becoming more human and difficult to detect study shows," E&T Engineering and Technology, https://eandt.theiet.org/ content/articles/2019/09/social-media-bots-are-becoming-more-human-and-diffic ult-to-detect-study-shows, September 2019.
18 Will Knight, "How to tell if you're talking to a bot," MIT Technology Review, https://www.technologyreview.com/2018/07/18/141414/how-to-tell-if-youre-talki ng-to-a-bot, July 2018.
19 Deirdre Breakenridge, "The Anatomy of the Apology," Spin Sucks Blog, https:// spinsucks.com/communication/the-anatomy-of-an-apology, March 2013.
20 Wikipedia, List of Fake News Sites, https://en.wikipedia.org/wiki/List_of_fake_ news_websites, September 2020
21 Melissa Fach, "How to Do a Reverse Image Search (Desktop and Mobile)," SEMRush Blog, https://www.semrush.com/blog/reverse-image-search, July 2020.

Chapter 3

Using Your Ethics in Cause Marketing

Would it surprise you to hear that millennials would prefer to work for, or work with, a company that supports social causes? Approximately 42% of millennials, as reported in Deloitte's eighth annual Millennial Survey, prefer to begin or deepen a relationship with a company whose products or services have a perceived positive impact on the environment. As a result, organizations are exploring ways to sponsor, lend financial support or engage in cause marketing. They are interested in aligning their brands with important causes to benefit the environment, help underserved populations, work with struggling economies due to natural disaster and any number of causes to help their communities. Associating your company with a good cause is an important step and one requiring careful consideration.[1]

However, when you make the decision to align, and to give support from the heart, when donating or working with a cause, you have to be ready to face the opportunity in a new media landscape. Are you prepared for the ups and downs of the communication and quite possibly your fair share of challenges should cause marketing mistakes occur? For every right move you make, and all the glowing praise you receive, there may be one wrong move sparking widespread criticism, especially when poor judgment or unethical behavior plays out in your marketing efforts. Whether your cause marketing is a part of your corporate social responsibility (CSR) program or stands alone, your values must always be front and center.

In the age of social media, you have a vast network of champions who are huge amplifiers of your cause. However, what happens when you have a lapse in judgment or there are missteps in cause marketing? You will be challenged by audiences, perhaps less forgiving of your brand. If you are a professional who has engaged in cause marketing in the past, then you may now find yourself in new territory. Think about what happens when brands engage in what they "think" is cause marketing, when it looks like they are jumping on a self-promotional bandwagon. You frequently witness this type of "support" during times of crisis, whether it is an act of terrorism, a region rocked by natural disaster or the world experiencing a global pandemic. Taking action through communication, during challenging or uncertain times, to promote your brand is never a good idea. The public recognizes when the "cause" in cause marketing is not from the heart. Brands learn very quickly the kind of backlash resulting from these types of marketing missteps.

As an Ethical Marketer, you realize a cause marketing initiative has to be an extension of the good judgment you would apply in any of your communication programs (marketing, PR, advertising, social media) through every media channel. However, there is a special lens you will need to apply with each interaction, message, and the engagement that results, in the spirit of supporting, funding and creating momentum for a cause. Investing your time, resources and energy into a program always has to be for the right reasons; because the underlying intent aligns with important values of the company, showcased by its team of Ethical Marketers.

The Q&A in this chapter focus on the ethical cause marketer and why companies have to let their values guide them. They have to adhere to ethical standards, which demonstrate the good intent and best practices when raising awareness and funds for a cause. The advice and stories in this chapter will help you to plot a careful course. As you do, you are also focusing on the cause, and the help part, and never losing sight of the people and organizations you are championing. Being fixated on the publicity and the spotlight for self-serving purposes is the approach to avoid.

When you are delivering communication from the heart it shows in your cause marketing results. You see the "Do Well by Doing Good" in the appreciation from the groups that benefit. Here are the questions and answers to help guide you.

Q38 How would you define cause marketing and why do we trust certain brands?

When I think of cause marketing the first thing that pops into my mind comes from a little wooden plaque on my desk. It says, "Do Well by Doing Good." This is one of the easiest ways to describe cause marketing. A company, or a brand product, creates a campaign, program or communications initiative for a dual purpose; for the betterment of society as they are also making a profit. Often, you will see a for-profit company team up with a non-profit organization for this for these reasons.

One brand that pops into my mind immediately is Toms. I shared in my book, *Answers for Modern Communicators*, how the Toms brand has built its business on the premise of "Do Well by Doing Good." They have a number of programs, which drive sales of their products and that are also aligned with non-profit organizations. As of the time of this writing, you can see on the Toms website how the company is "making progress with every purchase" and effective on April 1, 2020 giving one-third of their profit to their "Giving Partners that are responding to COVID-19—both at home and abroad."[2]

In the case of Toms, you see the ethical standards in their approach to cause marketing. Their values guide how they give, and they are recognized for this reason. Toms is transparent about who they are giving to, how much, and why they believe in their cause marketing collaborations. Establishing a track record for cause marketing helps a brand's customers to believe and support in the cause too. What develops is an underlying trust of the consumer.

For this same reason, I do not think twice when I'm at the checkout of my favorite supermarket, where we shop weekly. When the cashier asks me if I want to round up my payment to support a cause, it is an automatic, "Yes." I'm all in to support. At times, I am less familiar with the cause, yet I am still supportive. Why? Because it is the supermarket brand that I trust who is sharing the information with me. I trust my neighborhood supermarket, and based on my experience with them, I believe they are ethical and living up to the best standards in their cause marketing programs.

Q39 What are some problem areas to avoid in cause marketing?

Problem areas can appear in any area of marketing, not just cause marketing. However, common communication missteps and mishaps may stem from a lack of transparency with respect to your arrangement to support a cause, your intended charitable "give," and the goals of your campaign, all of which can become misleading to your customers.

When you set up a cause marketing program, it is your responsibility to be transparent in your communications. Customers should understand immediately how a charity or organization will benefit from your campaign, especially at the point of transaction. Your customer should be well informed with clarity of message and precise information, whether it is through an advertisement or a company representative. Customers should not have to ask how much your company is donating for each sale, the length of your campaign, any caps on their donations and any other information your company and legal team deem necessary.

All of these proactive measures are in an effort to prevent omitted or misleading communication about the nature of the cause and what you are delivering on its behalf. Also, on the short list of problems are the following:

- Keeping your brand in the spotlight instead of the charity. The result, unfortunately, after time and effort is expended, your customers will not lend their support to the cause. They don't see the value you are bringing to your cause marketing partner (perhaps only to your brand product in a self-serving way).
- Leading consumers to believe there is an endorsement of your product by the organization whose cause you are supporting. Brands have to be

careful not to mislead their customers (especially in the healthcare arena) with what looks like an unintended endorsement.

- Being very specific about the donation and not using ambiguous or unclear wording. Saying a portion of the proceeds of your product will be going to the cause is not precise enough. You have to share exactly what the donation is to be transparent and ethical in your approach.
- Aligning with brands who have your customers wondering, "Why you are partnering with a cause that is the complete opposite of your brand values or beliefs?" Cause marketing initiatives take careful consideration, so as not to dilute your mission and values, or confuse your customers.

Q40 What happens if you make a mistake in your cause marketing program that is not illegal, but you think it is unethical?

Just the fact you can spot a misstep is a step in the right direction. Now, it is time to use your voice and to correct the record. If you recognize a misstep, whether unethical or a mistake made in poor judgment, start with your team first. Share where the error occurred and the information you have researched or discovered, calling the situation into question. Be sure to have all your facts straight and sources ready and verified. You will want to present a solid case to your team, so you do not have to make any decisions alone. When you "Do Well by Doing Good" you are doing this with others who are actively working on and supporting your program.

As a team, you will need to alert your supervisors and or manager (who you report to directly) with any communication in error, inconsistent reporting and/or improper results of the cause marketing program, or backlash from the public, to name ways issues may surface. You will want everyone to be briefed, understanding what has transpired, why the action or actions are being called into question, and what documentation you have that conclude why the missteps are unethical and need to be corrected.

Then, up the chain it goes, so your leadership team can see if there are any steps, they need to address directly with your cause marketing partner. Of course, the misstep may remain with your team of Ethical Marketers in the marketing department, who are responsible for bringing the problem to the attention of your non-profit or the charitable organization you are supporting. Full transparency is always the best approach with your partner, so they can be ready to field any inquiries that will come through their communications channels.

Keeping the issue at bay, sweeping it under the carpet or wishing it will go away is not a suitable approach to dealing with unethical behavior, whether it was intentional or unintended. Having both your team and your cause marketing partner aware and ready to respond and/or take the necessary steps to change your program are the ethical steps you can set in motion to correct the situation.

In some cases, correcting the situation has to be done quickly. For example, MasterCard launched its cause marketing campaign to position itself as a "purveyor of social good" helping to feed starving children around the world. During the FIFA World Cup games, they made a pledge to feed thousands of children. For every football goal scored by two of the football greats, Messi and Neymar, MasterCard would feed 10,000 children.[3]

How quickly do you think it took their fans and influencers to start the backlash? On social media, not very long at all. The biggest question was why didn't MasterCard just feed starving children? Why did they need a cause marketing campaign? Was it just to stir up fan empathy and for their fans to take notice of this initiative? These are important question for all Ethical Marketers moving forward. MasterCard was able to navigate the backlash working closely with its partner the United Nations World Food Programme (WFP). **Note:** The Ethical Marketer would prefer not to be in this situation to begin with.

As an Ethical Marketer, you will want to think about the nature of your campaign. Pay careful attention to how your approach follows the "Do Well by Doing Good" mantra and how it will be seen by your market. Preventative steps are always better than having to clear up the missteps, which appear self-serving, unethical, and/or in poor judgment.

Q41 What are some good resources to learn more about ethics in cause marketing?

There is no shortage of resources to learn about ethics focused on any kind of marketing, including cause marketing. Here is a short list of action steps so you can find more specific cause marketing guidance:

- **Go to your network of marketers.** Whenever you have specific questions or want to hear advice you can just ask your "friends" on social media. If you are in a LinkedIn Group, or maybe it is your Twitter network, professionals on social media are more than willing to share their thoughts, helpful articles, white papers, case studies, websites and other online resources. Just like any other area of marketing, you don't have to guess or find the information on your own.
- **Ask a mentor.** Your mentors have years of experience and they are there to assist you. You would be surprised what a mentor has to share based on personal experience. When I shared a "truth to power" story in my book, *Answers for Modern Communicators*, I opened up the flood gates to other professionals who needed advice. Although not a

cause marketing situation, the example spoke to handling leadership and doing the right thing. Mentors are a great support system, whether it is in the area of cause marketing or any facet of your career.

- **Look to a professional association.** You do not have to be a member of PRSA to access all their helpful case studies and reports on ethics. Philanthropy and CSR are big areas and professionals need guidance. The PRSA website is a treasure trove of helpful information. You can also explore marketing associations to see if they have helpful guidance on cause marketing issues.
- **Find a professor.** I have several professors in my network who focus on ethics. They are happy when you reach out to ask a question. In the spirit of education, professors want all students (professionals are students too) acting and behaving ethically in their marketing programs. After all, it is in everyone's best interest. Professionals make up an industry and they represent that industry. If you do not know a professor, then build a Twitter list of ethics professors and start following them on social media. Tune into what they are sharing. Not only will you learn a lot, but you will also be able to build new relationships by asking them questions.
- **Do a Google search.** You might think that doing a Google search is overwhelming. However, use the right phrasing and keywords (don't forget to include the year to cut back on older resources) and you will pull up recent online articles, blogs, studies, reports and research papers on the search results pages. Then, if you find the author of the resource to be a knowledgeable expert, start following that person on social media. You may just end up with another mentor.

Q42 What happens if you are working with an organization (a good cause), and their communication lacks good judgment?

The secret to answering this question is to uncover the poor judgment before you actually engage with your new cause marketing partner. The role of the Ethical Marketer is to study communication, spot the signs, and decode the signals that may be troublesome. How have they coordinated in the past with other cause marketing partners? Were those campaigns guided by values and ethical behavior? What was the public's response to prior cause marketing campaigns they have launched? Do they have several long-term cause marketing partners? Long-term partners are a sign your new partner is doing well with their programs.

For a smaller company with only a few Ethical Marketers, assessing any challenges early on is easier. The Ethical Marketers are in "on the ground floor" and they are usually a part of the campaign ideation, negotiation and the agreement to engage. So, you may be wondering, what happens when you are on the team and it is a large enterprise? Perhaps you are not able to select the cause marketing partner and your charitable organization or non-profit is handed down to you by your leadership team. Then what? A similar practice mentioned earlier has to apply ... if you see something say something. It is critical for the team to be more vocal early on about any communication that enters the realm of poor judgment before it reaches full blown ethical issue in the public domain.

When you have a good cause then you have an opportunity to do well by doing good, and all parties benefit, including the consumer. They, too, feel great about participating in a well- orchestrated cause marketing program. When you are faced with a group that does not have the same checks and balances as you and does not place as much good judgment behind communication decisions, be the role model. As the role model, take shorter sprints in your program to evaluate and assess how you are doing as a team. Review often and be sure to course correct as you go along. Using an agile framework will help you not to go too far ahead in the campaign to realize many of your errors could have been prevented or corrected quickly.

Q43 How do you create change in cause marketing to prevent ethical missteps?

To create change is to be the change agent who is (1) knowledgeable and (2) vocal about what needs to change and why. If you know what makes a good cause marketing campaign, from the proper agreements and certifications to the legal steps to assure you are not in any jeopardy, then your cause marketing communication and the impact you create will reflect this knowledge and due diligence.

Going back to an answer earlier about the responsibility for ethical missteps, the team rises and falls together. Today, it is difficult to say, "I didn't know this," or "that is not my job" as you and your entire team witness the backlash on social media. The more the members of the team can be on the same page and supportive of a best-practices approach to cause marketing, the better the effort to prevent the missteps.

Being vocal as a team of Ethical Marketers (rather than just one lone marketer) can create change at any time. However, it would be in your team's best interest if the change comes as a united front before you engage in a new program. If you want to be the change agent, then you will set up the post evaluation of any of your cause marketing programs and involve your team of Ethical Marketers. Like any change management program, you are building your team, or coalition, with an urgency in your voice recognizing the importance of good ethical cause marketing practices. With an established urgency, one approach is to highlight and focus on any of the backlash from your previous cause marketing campaigns. Then, you will be able to launch a new vision for your programs, understanding what went wrong with previous programs. Looking back will help to create the action steps and communication that demonstrates good judgment moving forward. As a change agent, you are also a cheerleader rallying your team along the way, getting them excited about your next cause marketing program.

Q44 If you are ramping up for a cause marketing program, are there ways to educate your team quickly on ethics in communication?

Ramping up quickly does not mean you will ignore ethics and good judgment in your decision-making. What you are currently practicing with your team and the values and beliefs that guide you will still hold true. Yes, when programs are rushed, there are more chances to make mistakes and mistakes happen. However, correcting mistakes quickly and willingly, keeps you in good ethical standing.

Remember, ethics is your ability to do the right thing and to show your good judgment whether you are gearing up for a quicker campaign launch or you have months of planning ahead of you. Setting the parameters early on in the process, in terms of what you can and cannot do, as a part of your agreement will help. Your team has a responsibility to be ethical to your partner whether it is a charity or non-profit and they have a reciprocal responsibility.

Here is a breakdown of some of these responsibilities as partners. Ethical Marketers working for a brand need to make sure the following occurs with all communication:

- The approved messaging and imagery have proper sign off from your cause marketing partner. Who on their team has the approval power?
- The contact person at the charity or non-profit is available to answer questions and to provide communication guidance.
- Any areas of communication that have caused issues in the past should be reviewed and made known amongst all parties.
- Transparency in the way communication will filter through channels and who on your team handles regular touchpoints with customers.
- A contingency plan is in place should any issues or backlash occur. The think **AHEAD** approach works here as you can **Anticipate, Head-off** an issue, **Evaluate** the issue quickly, take **Action**, and **Determine** your success.

At the same time, your cause or charitable organization will need to take ownership over the following:

- Signing off in a timely manner on all campaign materials and branded communication.

- Being available when needed for regular calls or partner touchpoints during the campaign.
- Setting up a system to alert the ethical cause marketer to any changes or communication that they should be aware of during the length of the agreement.
- Being responsive online and on social media, if necessary, with respect to inquiries that can't be fielded by the ethical cause marketing team.

These are a handful of suggestions that can make a quick ramp-up more successful with both partners on board, setting expectations on how the campaign will run. The more the parties can stay united pre- and post-launch and have an "in this together" attitude, the better the program and the good judgment of a well-orchestrated team will prevail.

Q45 Do you have an example of a cause marketing campaign that seemed like a good idea at the time and then faced public backlash?

Mental Health Awareness is something that is near to my heart. When my stepdaughter, Noelle, passed away in 2018, she had studied psychology. Because she was a big advocate for breaking mental health stigma, we asked family and friends to donate to a mental health organization, National Alliance on Mental Illness (NAMI), in her memory. Asking people to give was tied directly to our purpose and values in remembrance of my stepdaughter.

Brands need to approach their cause marketing from a place of purpose and values. When Burger King launched its campaign #FeelYourWay during Mental Health Awareness Month, it appeared to have good intentions around an important topic. However, here is where their cause marketing efforts suffered in the eyes of the public.

First, Burger King's mission did not reflect the mental health and well-being of its customers. Its mission statement talks about good quality food, served quickly in a friendly environment. In the eyes of Burger King's customers, it was a bit of a stretch to focus on mental health. There was a disconnect and the comments on social media, especially Twitter, did not reflect the campaign focus and the company's overall focus. Some tweets were kind, pointing out that it was fine for Burger King to support when people feel unhappy. However, they didn't understand why a fast-food company was capitalizing on marketing mental health issues.

Then came another kind of backlash that Burger King did not expect from their cause marketing campaign. Past Burger King employees joined the conversation to share how Burger King did not provide mental health insurance. One former employee wrote in his tweet sharing his #truestory. From his experience and words, when he asked his boss at Burger King for a day off to see his therapist, the boss allegedly replied, "Either you work the hours you're scheduled, or you're fired." The message in the tweet (whether captured accurately or not by the former employee) certainly did not match the intended cause marketing messages and the campaign to support mental health awareness.[4]

Marketing teams come up with creative campaigns all the time. You, as the Ethical Marketer. and ethical cause marketer, have to really think past the idea to visualize how all parts will be received by your customers and other stakeholders. Aligning to the right cause based on your values is one of the first questions you should ask, so you avoid becoming the next Burger King in question or cause marketing #Fail on social media, regardless of your good intentions.

Q46 If there are ethical challenges that come with cause marketing, then why should you bother building out these types of programs?

Why should I ride a bicycle if I may fall off my bike?

Why should I be in a relationship if I can get hurt?

Why should I write this book if I am not sure people will buy it?

Why should I launch this product if it could be a flop?

Why? For the fun, the passion, the thrill, the creation, and for a really good cause. There are more reasons why people engage in activities and take risks. How would you answer the questions above? Would you take a little risk to enjoy your life more, for something you felt strongly about and for a purpose that was driving you forward? Chances are you would say, "Yes!"

Even if you fell off that bicycle or got bruised in a relationship, you would still get up and do it again. There is no holding back passion, and, hopefully, it is the same when it comes to cause marketing. Your passion and purpose are greater than anticipation over the challenges or the bumps and bruises along the way. Of course, like the questions with the examples, you take preventative measures. You wear a helmet on your bike, and you select your relationships more carefully.

The same goes for cause marketing. You prepare by selecting the right partner with a well thought out program that is less likely to pose ethical issues. Here are a few pointers to help you, if you are in a position to select your cause marketing charity or non-profit to give you that ounce of prevention:

- Your cause marketing partner shares a similar culture to you. Their organization is also aligned to your values. For example, if truth, integrity, accuracy, respect, and fairness are your standards and theirs too, then you have a match.

- You are able to support their business goals through a cause marketing program. They need fundraising for their research, and you are the partner experienced in these types of programs. Their needs and your experience matters.
- Not only are the brands aligned but also the expectations are in alignment too. Your partner sees realistic objectives and goals. You want to avoid a situation where a cause marketing partner expects you to raise $100,000.00 from the proceeds of product purchases, when realistically you were focused on raising $10,000.00.
- A cause marketing partner must be available and responsive and willing to work closely with you. Your partner has to share in just as much passion as you and your team. When both partners have a genuine commitment to "the cause" it really shows.
- Your cause marketing partner is ready to put the initiative in writing with a contract so there are no loose ends. When you spell out your partnership carefully there is less room for error and miscommunication on the scope of your effort.

Q47 As an Ethical Marketer, how do you know the best cause to support?

Supporting a cause is based on passion. There are two sides to this coin: the passion of your people and the passion of your customers. Both are important.

However, because you are one culture and one brand that attracts a certain type of customer, the passion will most likely be unanimous. In this case selecting the best cause or the most appropriate cause comes down to the people, in general. Here is where staying close to your stakeholders really matters. I have seen far too many executives try to decide what the brand is about and what it means to the important stakeholders they need to engage, including their own people.

Today, brands are built by your stakeholders. If you do not know the important causes of your own people or the causes aligned to your customers preferences, then it is time to find out. Selecting the right cause marketing partner is a great investment, which requires people, time and resources. You do not want to select these partners based on what the boardroom thinks. Get closer to your people and what they think.

Companies are creating employee branding surveys and asking these questions as a part of their brand experience with their companies. They can also create discussions around important causes in their internal social networks. Leaders making decisions about the partners just have to listen to what is being shared in their slack communities or whatever discussion forums they have in place.

After the passion part is fulfilled, it is on to the business end where ethics often come into question. Other considerations will focus on how your partner structures a cause-marketing partnership. For instance, if there are registration requirements, legal contracts that need to be put into place, and the transparency and reporting requirements necessary for your efforts.

From passion to ethical business practices, the right partner will have to check all of these boxes.

Q48 What is a really good example of a brand that gives, and also takes an ethical approach?

I'm not a big potato chip fan, however, Frito-Lay really had my attention when they debuted their 60-second commercial and boldly stated, "This is not about brands, it's about people." At a time of crisis, during a global pandemic, when people are uncertain about their jobs, food for their families, the state of the economy, and as of this writing, if we will be social distancing through the rest of 2020, Frito-Lay wants to highlight their "philanthropy not chips."

From a cause marketing standpoint, the commercial hits several of the key components for a good campaign. First, Frito-Lay is recognizing times are hard for people during COVID-19. They are not asking their consumers and constituents to purchase for a donation. They are demonstrating their philanthropy and making donations on their own. The video highlights several ways Frito-Lay is giving to people and businesses across the country. From creating new jobs and donating $15 million for relief efforts to providing 20 million nutritious meals for at risk students, funding mobile health clinics and offering COVID-19 screenings, the imagery is all about helping people.

Interestingly, as they distinguish themselves as a brand that helps, lifts and gives, they also set themselves apart from the brands that just change their logos (which some brands do to reflect their philanthropy or cause marketing efforts) and they are not asking people to "donate for us." From the heart, they are taking the initiative to "Do Well by Doing Good" all by themselves. The end of their commercial has a Call to Action (CTA), offering a link to the fritolay.com/action website. Viewers can find out more about the company's proactive COVID-19 response. They also see how this is only the beginning with respect to the impact Frito-Lay will create.

Is Frito-Lay also raising awareness for its brand? Yes. Will Frito-Lay sell products during its focus on people and giving as a result of Coronavirus? Yes. However, as they do, they are still doing really well by doing good, every step of the way.

The Marketing Experts "Weigh In" on Ethical Guidance

Cause Marketing Can Be a Win-Win Situation for Both the For-Profit Business and the Non-Profit Organization

By Holly Golcher, Higher Education Administrator

This topic brings me back to eight years ago when I was writing my Master's thesis and obtaining my Graduate Certificate in the Management of Non-profit Organizations. It is rewarding when we realize that businesses and organizations can work individually, or together, and learn from one another while enhancing society in both an economical and ethical way. As long as the businesses and organizations are using good judgment, they can become more profitable while helping a noble cause. When we stop and think about it, cause marketing is everywhere around us, and that's a great thing!

Open your computer or turn on the television and you are bound to find cause marketing. Some examples I am fond of are soap commercials with women of all colors, shapes and sizes, trying to eliminate a certain body image that women strive for while putting their mental and physical health at risk. Another is transgender women modeling the latest makeup line or lingerie. Or a jewelry brand marketing same-sex marriage and advertising wedding bands as interchangeable for both men and women to wear. As a consumer, I take pride in buying from these brands.

These companies are trying to be inclusive and market their products to buyers by sending a message that is welcoming to everyone. Yet, I know that not everyone shares the same appreciation for these campaigns as I do, and that some might view them as not relatable, distasteful, or even unethical. We all live by different ethics so it makes sense that society will never fully agree on any one topic.

I recently purchased some popcorn online that I was so excited to try because I had heard great things regarding the varieties of flavors offered, the ingredients, and the specific cause the brand supported. Each bag states that 3% of proceeds goes toward allergy and asthma research, which I will gladly support because as someone who works in a non-profit research institution I am elated to see and support my fellow research institutes. Of course, as consumers, we make purchases that are best for our families and if we can help contribute to society by supporting brands that join themselves with organizations that promote a good cause, then we intuitively show pride in our purchases and in return, the products bring a sense of joy. Whether you are a big company that sponsors the Olympics, or you are a local hair salon joining forces with an organization to save water and clean the ocean, then to me, both are equally meaningful.

Unfortunately, unethical cause marketing exists and may be apparent to some but not others. Ultimately, it is up to the consumer to do their homework to see how truthful the marketing campaigns are. For instance, a company advertises that "a portion" of your food purchase goes towards a foundation, but after a few clicks on their website and reading the small print you come to find that this multi-million-dollar company donating "a portion," is really one-tenth of 1% of sales. This could be viewed as misleading to consumers because my perception would be that more than one cent for every ten dollars spent actually goes to supporting the cause. On the other hand, one-tenth of 1% is still better than nothing, right? If consumers want to find companies that donate larger percentages of their sales to organizations, then they will do their research.

With social media sitting in everyone's back pocket it is easy to spread good or bad news. I personally use social media to learn about products and services because many people are willing to share their thoughts and opinions with friends and family online when it comes to reviews on brands that utilize cause marketing. With people flocking to scandals and the "cancel culture" we are currently experiencing it can be extremely difficult to recover from a bad campaign. Therefore, companies' and organizations' marketing and management teams need to be sure that they identify potential repercussions if they make a claim towards a cause that they are not truly supporting as advertised.

At the end of the day, it is up to the for-profit businesses and non-profit organizations to work individually or together in the most ethical ways possible. There are many great marketing campaigns geared towards supporting some great causes. We all contribute what we can in our own way, and cause marketing can help grow businesses and organizations. As a consumer, buying products that satisfy my needs while also bettering society does show that one person and one purchase at a time can make a difference and help change the world!

Ethics in Cause Marketing

By Mark W. McClennan, APR, Fellow PRSA, General Manager of C+C's Boston Office

Cause marketing is advocating for something bigger than yourself and your brand. It is going beyond self-interest and simply selling more widgets to actually addressing issues that matter to society.

Purpose today matters more than ever. A 2020 Edelman study[5] found that 50% of consumers say a brand helping out is a must for earning or keeping their trust. The survey shows that people will hold brands accountable for their actions. Additionally, 52% of those asked said brands will have to protect people to earn or keep their trust, and 71% said the companies that prioritize profits over people will lose their trust forever. While I personally think forever is a bit over the top, it will have a lasting impact, particularly with younger customers.

Unfortunately, some executives are still resistant to the ideals behind cause marketing and do not want to substantively align their brands with something bigger. If you need to convince a skeptical executive, I would turn to the Business Roundtable statement in 2019[6] that said stakeholder value, not shareholder value, is the ultimate purpose of a corporation. One of the key stakeholders for any corporation is the society in which they operate. To make an even sharper point, a 2018 Conference Board/Ernst & Young Global Leadership Forecast[7] has the most compelling financial evidence for the skeptical executive: Purposeful companies outperform the stock market by 42%. Beyond the moral imperative, brands do good by doing good.

While a comprehensive overview of the power, potential and pitfalls of cause marketing is beyond the purview of a chapter in a book, there are a few things to highlight.

TWO TOP ISSUES WITH CAUSE MARKETING

Determining a good cause. A 2018 USC Annenberg study[8] found that while 60% of communicators want to engage on societal issues, 60% of CEOs are less likely to engage. While this has likely shifted due to COVID-19 and other events of 2020, a quandary remains. There are so many causes out there that matter, how does a brand determine when to engage and when not to engage? Will your efforts help the cause or dilute the focus and funding for a cause?

For brands, effective, ethical cause marketing is found in the causes that are related to your purpose and mission. You should prioritize them over other issues and align your cause work around historic inequities. The causes tend to come from issues impacting your business and your stakeholders, or something personal to your company. Your brand should not be like a soccer team of seven-year-olds, chasing back and forth after the moving ball. Pick a few issues that are relevant, commit to them for a sustained campaign and invest in them to drive impact. To do otherwise is inauthentic and will dilute your efforts and results. Additionally, large companies should be transparent about the impacts they've had on communities in the past and use cause marketing to infuse resources into those communities.

The ethical perils of greenwashing. Environmental causes have been growing in importance over the past decade, but so has greenwashing. Underwriters Laboratories (UL) released a study in 2010 that states 95% of eco-friendly claims are based on irrelevant, weak, or non-existent data.[9] There are a number of common fallacies, including the unethical hidden trade-offs. Paper from a sustainable-harvested forest is not necessarily superior. Other important environmental issues in the paper-making process, such as greenhouse gas emissions and water pollution, may be as important if not more so.

Other issues include vagueness (i.e. claiming a product is better when it is all natural when it contains arsenic and uranium). While accurate, it is misleading by ignoring health issues. Another pitfall is companies making irrelevant claims ("our product is CFC-free" ... when CFCs are banned). Additionally, consumers are becoming more skeptical about green claims. Is Quantas really going to be Net Zero when it comes to carbon emissions by 2050? I am skeptical.

It is great if the environment and green issues are an integral part of your purpose, just be careful of the slippery ethical slope on which some of those claims may be based.

HOW DO YOU AVOID MAKING MISTAKES?

While ethics and values should be central to any marketing and communication efforts, it is more important in cause marketing than any other activity, except perhaps financial reporting. Yet it is easy to make accidental missteps. In the Disinformation Age where alleged "facts" are just a Google search away, marketers must trust but verify by double checking all claims to make sure they are relevant, defensible, and clear. They need to make sure green claims educate consumers rather than confuse them. The legal department is your friend and it is important to work with them to validate claims.

For most businesses, the cause they are supporting is not their primary purpose. But there are advocacy groups and non-profits that have the cause as the primary purpose. They can be a great resource and ally. You should work to build bridges with them, look at their data and see how you may be of assistance.

In the end, for cause marketing to be ethical and effective, it comes down to the same issues we face in any other marketing efforts: use your company's mission and values as your North Star; have regular ethics discussions with your team and partners; and look to see what other brands involved in the cause are doing well (and not so well). Clearly define what you will accept and what you will not accept from employees, partners and your supply chain.

Cause marketing is not a cost center. It is core to an organization's purpose and integral to being a part of a larger community. Ethical cause marketing is effective and pays dividends for business both in terms of how your brand can improve society, but also in how well you sleep at night.

Cause Marketing and Staying True to Your Brand

By Shonali Burke, President & CEO, Shonali Burke Consulting, Inc.

Several years ago, I ran the public relations function for the ASPCA (the American Society for the Prevention of Cruelty to Animals). As you might imagine, it was simultaneously exciting, challenging and rewarding to be the brand steward for the country's oldest animal protection organization (and second oldest such organization in the world). I learned so much during my time there, I could probably write an entire book on it … but that's not what *this* book is about!

One of the many challenges that non-profit organizations can face is that of visibility, and getting their voice heard in an extremely crowded marketplace. Thanks in no small part to the incredible work my team did, that was *not* one of the ASPCA's problems. In fact, particularly as we elevated the brand's awareness and reputation among our publics, we were in the enviable position of far more brands approaching us with cause marketing proposals, than those we approached with partnership ideas. One such initiative was ASPCA-branded pet insurance.

By way of background, the concept of pet insurance is much older than you probably think it is; the first pet insurance policy was written in Sweden in 1890.[10] But it took almost a century to make its way to the United States; VPI (Veterinary Pet Insurance), as it was then known (it rebranded as Nationwide in 2014), sold the first pet insurance policy to television's most iconic dog, "Lassie."[11]

I had been at the ASPCA just a few months when I was brought into the pet insurance discussion, which the organization was (justifiably) excited about, as it had the potential not just to extend the Society's brand, but also add to its revenue sources as well. Up until that point in my career, the only experience I had with insurance was being covered by it! That certainly changed by the time we launched the product, and it was a great introduction to ethical cause marketing.[12]

Here's some of what I learned:

I YOUR NON-PROFIT'S BRAND IS EXTREMELY VALUABLE. DON'T DISCOUNT IT.

The reason that a corporate entity is interested in partnering with you in the first place is because it wants to extend its market share by aligning with your cause (hence "cause marketing"). After all, chances are that you're not the only non-profit pursuing your specific mission, right? So, the corporate partner could, potentially, partner with any number of non-profits. Why, then, are they coming to you?

Of course, the partnership needs to be viable for both entities; that goes without saying. But I think far too many non-profits get a bit overawed, perhaps even intimidated, by the thought of this "big" corporate entity wanting to partner with it. Don't! You have as much right to be at the negotiating table as they do. So, do what is in your, and your stakeholders', best interest.

2 ARE YOUR CORPORATE PARTNER'S AND YOUR BRAND VALUES CONSISTENT?

This brings me to my second point. When evaluating cause marketing opportunities, you really have to think long and hard about whether or not your, and your partner's, brand values are aligned and consistent.

In the ASPCA's case, they absolutely were. After all, the Society was literally founded to protect animals and to provide the means for the prevention of cruelty towards them. It's pretty easy to see how lending its name and brand to a pet insurance product—which held significant potential to ease the financial burden that pet parents face (and I learned firsthand just *how* much pet insurance can help!)—was extremely consistent with its mission of keeping animals safe.[13]

But if that is not the case with a cause marketing venture you are considering, think long and hard before entering into that venture. Alienating your donor base because they think you are selling out will do significant damage to your brand, its ability to pursue its mission and, ultimately, to its revenue sources both from individual donors as well as other potential corporate partners.

3 NEVER COMPROMISE ON YOUR AUDIENCE'S TRUST.

When we started planning the launch of ASPCA Pet Health Insurance, we knew we'd have to clearly explain why this was a good thing for not just the organization, but for America's pet parents and, ultimately, pet population.[14] But insurance is, at the best of times, difficult to understand. While pet insurance is more common today, in 2006 it was still considered pretty unusual. So, we did a lot of groundwork in explaining how it works, what would and wouldn't be covered (which has likely changed over time), and so on. We wanted to make sure that our constituents didn't feel the organization was out to make a quick buck and were very clear about what they were signing up for. After all, they trusted us. And our topmost priority was to ensure that we didn't betray that trust.

So, we worked overtime to develop, and communicate, our messaging, whether through the media, social media (though it was nascent at the time), email and direct marketing, web copy and, most importantly, to employees as well.

Cause marketing is a big part of non-profit revenue generation. But at the end of the day, if it is not built on an ethical foundation, no amount of revenue will mitigate the potential damage to your brand from a breach of trust. Keep that at the center of your cause marketing, and you'll grow not just your brand, but your market share, positioning, and thought leadership as well.

Notes

1 The Deloitte Global Millennial Survey 2020, https://www2.deloitte.com/global/en/pages/about-deloitte/articles/millennialsurvey.html, September 2020.
2 Toms Website, Global Giving Fund—COVID-19, https://www.toms.com/us/impact.html, September 2020.
3 Stephen Lepitak, "'The worst marketing I've ever seen' – Mastercard's World Cup children's meals campaign stirs debate," The Drum, https://www.thedrum.com/news/2018/06/02/the-worst-marketing-ive-ever-seen-mastercards-world-cup-childrens-meals-campaign, June 2018.
4 Amanda Milligan, "Burger King Teaches You How to do Cause Marketing Wrong," Content Marketing Institute, https://contentmarketinginstitute.com/2019/06/cause-marketing-wrong, June 2019.
5 Thomas Moore, "Brands better step up during pandemic: Edelman Trust Barometer special," PR Week, March 2020, https://www.prweek.com/article/1678756/brands-better-step-during-pandemic-edelman-trust-barometer-special; Richard Edelman, "Trust Barometer Special Report: Brand Trust and the Coronavirus Pandemic," https://www.edelman.com/research/covid-19-brand-trust-report, March 2020.
6 Business Roundtable, "Business Roundtable Redefines the Purpose of a Corporation to Promote 'An Economy That Serves All Americans'," https://www.businessroundtable.org/business-roundtable-redefines-the-purpose-of-a-corporation-to-promote-an-economy-that-serves-all-americans, August 2019.
7 Pontefract Group, "Purpose-Driven Companies Outperform the Financial Markets by 42 Percent," https://www.danpontefract.com/purpose-driven-companies-outperform-the-financial-markets-by-42-percent, March 2019.
8 USC Center for Public Relations, "Relevance Report 2021," https://annenberg.usc.edu/research/center-public-relations/relevance-report, October 2020.
9 terrachoice/UL, "The Sins of Greenwashing: Home and Family Edition 2010," http://faculty.wwu.edu/dunnc3/rprnts.TheSinsofGreenwashing2010.pdf, 2010.
10 Karsten Strauss, "Insurance for Pets Goes Public," Forbes, https://www.forbes.com/sites/karstenstrauss/2014/07/18/insurance-for-pets-goes-public/#3bb46d8378ef, July 2014.
11 Nationwide Website, "We Put Members and Their Pets First," https://www.petinsurance.com/we-invented, August 2020.
12 Insurance News Center Online, "ASPCA Launches 'ASPCA Pet Health Insurance'," https://insurancenewsnet.com/oarticle/ASPCA-Launches-ASPCA-Pet-Health-Insurance-a-161487#.XvD_CpNKgc8, October 2006.
13 ASPCA Website, About Us Section, https://www.aspca.org/about-us, August 2020.
14 ASPCA Pet Health Insurance Online, https://www.aspcapetinsurance.com, August 2020.

Taking Ethics to Media
Interviews and Appearances

Business professionals spend time and resources on media training. They show up to their interviews with their talking points and practiced techniques. They are ready to manage any type of interview, from the softball features to the hardball, real-time questions and opportunities. However, today, it is **not** enough to simply show up with just your prepared messaging and your interview agenda. You have to be ready to go well beyond the "why" of your appearance and prepare to engage in discussions that are not always easy to navigate. Look at some of the topics in the news from politics and racial injustice to the economy, a global pandemic and affordable healthcare. Yet, no matter how tough, toxic or manipulated the conversations get, you have to keep your eye on the ball. Of course, staying focused means having your ethics and values, emotional intelligence, good sense and wise judgment with you, from start to finish.

Just because you may "feel" well-equipped does not necessarily mean you can predict the media person's agenda, or how your sound bites will play out on social media. However, what you can count on is your own ability to be present with your good intentions, and to know what you can and should discuss. Your goal is to deliver the truth, be accurate and informative, and bring communications transparency to the people receiving the information you share. Your job, as the expert in an interview, is to always think responsibly about the audience you are serving; being sure to help people and not confuse or harm them.

When you reach expert interview status, the megaphone is in your hands, so you can amplify a story through the media. There is an opportunity and a responsibility. Yet, you may be watching your favorite interview programs or reading your favorite publications and wondering what has happened to the good sense and the responsibility in communication. Perhaps you are seeing less ethics and values play out in media interviews, as more ego and hubris take center stage. Are you seeing an increase in healthy public discourse or anger and polarized opinions on social media? What is an Ethical Marketer to do?

You can start now with your interview preparation and the thoughts, feelings and behavior you take into your interviews. After all, you know that ethics and good judgment need to go everywhere you go, especially to media interviews and appearances. Whether you are the person interviewing or you are training someone else, it is time to put the ethics back into media by showing up, standing up for your values, and by demonstrating ethical behavior with every interaction. Of course, you may be thinking, "How can one Ethical Marketer do this alone and make a difference?"

Well, it takes one to start, and many to join in the cause, and then an army of many more to follow and consciously amplify ethical communication through media. Together you can propagate the helpful information. The interview and its aftermath break down into an equation that has a few parts.

- **Part I:** You begin with the interview preparation and commit to taking ethical "steps" regardless of the questions asked, or the bias of the outlet, or even your own bias.
- **Part II:** You deliver information from a place of clear thinking and open-mindedness. You are present and your open mindset helps you to share your values and be reflective of others during the discussion.
- **Part III:** Post interview, you will take the time necessary to review your interview and investigate how what you have shared showed up and played out through the media and on social media.
- **Part IV:** You will address your interview and continue to share helpful information on the topic, paying careful attention to the social media "echo chamber." The echo chamber delivers what you want to hear and see, based on your own bias and behavior, that is being tracked by a social network algorithm. Make sure you step out of your own lane to review different perspectives from various outlets and communities and be ready to correct the misinformation when necessary and to add objectively to a discussion.

Ethical Marketers can seize any interview opportunity and uphold their responsibility of presenting what is considered accurate, fair, truthful, and in good faith in their interview conversations. However, as of the time of this writing, the media has taken a beating in the ethics department and so have the professionals who have interviewed through broadcast channels, print, online publications and blogs, and on podcasts and livestreaming shows. Because media is one of the quickest ways to get your message out, it is also a wake-up call for professionals to focus on ethics and the different parts of the equation. You want to go into every media encounter guided by your values (your Ethics GPS) and good judgment.

The following Q&A will help you address different situations you may face as an Ethical Marketer as you, your executives or your teams share thought leadership and lend a voice to important industry topics through select media channels. The public benefits when you uphold ethics and values in every part of the media interview equation, from what you prepare and what you say to what the people around you share.

Q49 What happens if you are asked to inflate numbers for your media interviews?

Do you remember President Trump's inauguration on January 20, 2017? There was quite a bit of debate and angry banter about the size of the crowd at the National Mall in Washington, DC that day. Did more people attend the event compared to our last President's inauguration or were there fewer people? According to Wikipedia, the number of attendees was somewhere between 300,000 and 600,000, noting this was about one-third less than President Obama. Why would it matter if President Trump or his then-Press Secretary Sean Spicer created the image of a huge crowd, the largest ever, one far greater than the media was reporting?[1] For the sake of argument, let us say that the number of people attending President Trump's swearing in was considerably smaller. Whether it was the rainy weather preventing citizens from attending or people just decided not to come out that day, why would saying an inflated number rather than a more accurate accounting, be a test of ethics?

When people steer away from the truth it starts with a small white lie. White lies are the beginning of making it easier **not** to tell the truth, especially if these white lies become accepted as commonplace.[2] According to a study in Nature Neuroscience, when you tell white lies you are helping your brain adapt to dishonesty. Today, it might be inflating a harmless number. However, what happens when that number becomes a little more important … it is the amount of money you say you have donated to a charity, or it is the number of troops you are taking out of a war zone, or it becomes the number of people who are sick and dying, or not affected, from a virus during a health pandemic? The example, of course, is not an opinion, yet an instance of how the inflated numbers can grow from a harmless stretch to a much more serious situation where the truth can save lives.

According to the study mentioned, "what begins as small acts of dishonesty can escalate into larger transgressions." As an Ethical Marketer, if you recognize that a white lie is viewed as a small act of dishonesty, would you inflate the numbers, or would you recommend an executive on your team to do the same?[3]

Now, you get to decide.

Q50 What happens if you exaggerate a situation, stretch the truth or even flat out lie in a media interview?

Hyperbole is an exaggeration. However, when does it cross the line? It is not quite a lie, which clearly has no business in a media interview. When you knowingly misrepresent the truth, you are demonstrating unethical behavior. The fact that you are broadcasting misrepresentation of the truth through the media, with a far greater reach, than if you were delivering the same information to a group of colleagues (which is still wrong) makes your actions more offensive.

Exaggeration has consequences and that is where this ethics answer begins. How many times have you witnessed exaggeration in storytelling? What were the consequences? In the case of Brian Williams, former anchor of the NBC program, The Nightly News with Brian Williams, there were repercussions to an exaggerated story. When he misrepresented events covering the Iraq war, NBC suspended him for sixth months. It took a couple of years for Williams to resurface on MSNBC as the host of The 11th Hour with Brian Williams. However, Williams apologized and was accountable for the situation. The reputation damage was repaired. Even though journalists and the professionals who interview can look at what happened as an example of the consequences, there are so many instances of extreme exaggeration that go unnoticed or unchecked.

Here is an easy rule to follow ... stick to the facts in your interview. In my experience, I have noticed that executives who are under pressure and caught off guard with a question may use hyperbole when they are not prepared to answer. The exaggeration comes from a place of filling in words and making the answer appear more important. The specifics, which should be shared, are either unknown or cannot be shared. When people are under pressure they tend to embellish or misremember events.

In order to avoid hyperbole, you have to identify the range from human nature and often poor judgment to a more dangerous and serious commentary. Although not in reference to media interviews, but rather company interviews, back in 2003, the Society of Human Resource Management (SHRM) stated that more than 50% of all job applicants used inaccurate information on their resumes.[4] Surely, the hurt in this instance falls back on the candidate who does not receive the call back interview. A quick Google search can tell you a lot about who you are really speaking with and how much experience the person has. However, you cross the line when you misrepresent career qualifications. For instance, in the healthcare industry, you can affect the lives of others and/or harm people directly. As an Ethical Marketer, although human nature may be to stretch and embellish in storytelling, the lesson is to just stick to the story—the facts—and avoid exaggeration in your interviews.

Of course, when it comes to flat-out lying, think of the last time someone lied to you. Do you count on them for information and do you have a good relationship? Lying is unethical and, depending on the situation, can also get you into legal trouble.

Q51 If you make a mistake in an interview, is there a way to clear up the record or update your statement?

Absolutely, because mistakes happen, and it is up to you to correct the record. When you interview with a journalist, blogger, podcaster, TV host, etc., there is usually a final question. "Is there anything else you would like to share?" If you know you have made an error related to a statistic, or you offered information about a date, an event or a person that might not accurately have been portrayed, then this is your opportunity to set the record straight. You can simply state that what you referred to earlier may not be entirely accurate or exact. Offering the information post-interview and getting it to your media contact quickly is also appreciated. Reputable media is looking for your truthful account and will thank you for being forthright.

Your goal should always be to deliver information with transparency, truth, accuracy and responsibility. The longer you wait to set the record straight, the worse it can get for you and your company. However, there may be instances if you are "live" in an interview broadcast and the incorrect part of the interview ends up as your sound bite used in real-time on social media, from short video clips to memes, and what is commented on by other experts in the news. At this point, you should continue to correct the record with the facts; restating them through your own channels and through the channels of your influential social media friends will help too.

When you make a mistake, or information is taken out of context, be sure to pinpoint it quickly and directly. Then, fix it swiftly and gracefully. Whether you catch the error in real-time, or you realize it in hindsight, you still want to correct the record. The effort you put into the correction will be appreciated by the journalists whose credibility, at times, rests in the hands of the people they interview and the stories they share.

Correcting the record can help you to keep your media relationships strong and your integrity intact.

Q52 In a crisis, are self-serving messages considered unethical? Or is it considered poor judgment?

You can answer this question by breaking down the pillars of ethics. The Arthur W. Page Society has five pillars, which are telling the truth, doing no harm, always doing good, respecting privacy, and being fair and responsible.[5]

Now, think about what happens when crisis strikes and people are confused, scared and quite possibly hurt. They are in need of information quickly. They are looking for information that comes with accuracy, transparency, and helpful instruction, all in a timely manner. If you are a company watching a crisis play out, whether it is affecting your industry, the market, your region or anywhere around the world, what constitutes doing the right thing? There are companies that set out to help in uncertain times. For instance, during the Coronavirus global pandemic, a number of companies offered help immediately and they came from a place of "doing good." There was a running list of companies curated by *Insider*, showing the brands that give products or donations to people affected by COVID-19. These companies ranged from food and clothing brands to beauty, home, parenting and pet companies.[6]

What do all of these companies have in common? They offer their help, aid, and services to benefit people affected by the crisis. They are "doing good" in a transparent way and they are not looking for profit. Their "gifts" come at a time when people really need extra support, well beyond what their families, friends, employers or even their communities and their government can offer. However, on the opposite end of the spectrum, there are those companies that fall into the self-serving news category. They approach the "help" from a place of publicity and being in the spotlight. Their "give" is set up to make a profit, which is both unethical and in poor judgment. A word comes to mind when brands jump on a news story, whether it is for the right or the wrong reasons. In communications circles, it is known as newsjacking.[7]

Back in 2012, Hurricane Sandy wreaked havoc on the New England coastline. Companies had a choice as to how they were going to share their "give" or charitable gifts with the public. Duracell rolled out with a portable power station where people could recharge their electronic devices. Being a resident of New Jersey and in close proximity to the shore, which suffered the eye of the storm, our power was out for almost two weeks. Duracell was giving a much-needed service while raising awareness. Their "give" came with responsibility and good judgment. However, one brand called out negatively for its "give" was American Apparel who offered a 20% discount to customers affected by Hurricane Sandy. This "give" was for profit and deemed unethical by the public.[8]

Be sure to test your communication at all times, especially during a crisis, against those five pillars and you will know quickly what is ethical and if your decision-making shows good judgment.

Q53 If your band makes a mistake and you upset your customers, can you make it right through the media?

Yes, you can correct the record through the media. However, you will need more than one type of media or channel depending on how far and wide the communication travels.

When o.b. Tampons had to remove their products from store shelves as a result of supply issues, their customers were very unhappy. This equaled about 65,000+ annoyed women. The company knew it and decided to use the media to send personalized apology songs to every one of their loyal customers. Here is where the media makes a difference. Customers began sharing their personalized apologies from o.b. Tampons' parent company.[9] As a result, the efforts were also picked up by media outlets focusing on how the company was genuinely sorry and wanted to do what was right for their customers. In this case, the media helped to make an unhappy situation better.

Airbnb is another example of a company quick to make an apology to customers by understanding the power of the media, getting their "I'm sorry" across the right way. When Airbnb was accused of discrimination, the CEO did not run away from the accusations but instead addressed them head on through the media. Airbnb also created a new company policy, which a took a harder stance against discrimination, and they also launched an inclusion campaign to action what the policy stated. At the time of this writing, their YouTube video "We Accept" has over 5.1 million views.[10]

Toyota also made a very public apology through the media after 90 people were killed as a result of defects and they had to recall several million cars. Although they did not take accountability for the defects right from the start, when they decided to make their apology, it went far and wide. They created personal apologies (condolence letters). They also invested in an advertising campaign in major newspapers to address how they did not live up to safety standards and what they were going to do to focus on safety issues moving forward. Of course, executives also interviewed on news programs to support the apology tour.[11]

Even if you are watching social media play out about your brand, product or program missteps, you can still use media to thoughtfully and with good intentions set the record straight. Of course, it is highly advised to be accountable quickly and not wait for the $1.2 Billion settlement or a probe by the Department of Justice (in the case of Toyota).[12]

Q54 What happens if your company wants you to blame everyone (including the media) for your organization's or your leaders' missteps? Should you?

Blame is the opposite of accountable leadership. Unfortunately, corporate and government leaders are finding it is much easier to blame than to find a path to accountability. At the same time, blame does not help the situation. Blame does not allow the professionals or officials involved to fix what is actually going wrong, or to prevent more harm and the issue from happening again, when no one wants to take responsibility.

There was a lot of finger pointing around the BP oil spill in April 2010. As the media shared tragic photos of wildlife and baby ducks covered in black oil, BP's executives were not taking accountability. Tony Hayward, CEO of BP, shared in a news article how the spill was not their company's drilling rig, or a part of their process or their equipment. Although, BP was willing to take responsibility for the cost of the clean-up, they were not directly owning up to their part of the catastrophe. Instead, BP pointed fingers at Transocean Limited, an offshore drilling company. It did not take long for the media and the public to learn that the US District Court Judge presiding over the case determined BP carried 67% fault in the oil spill.[13]

Another example of finger pointing occurred during a Bloomberg media interview when the CEO of Lululemon, Chip Wilson, blamed his own customers for the company's "sheer pants" problem. The brand recalled many of their black yoga pants because they had become too sheer. Rather than taking accountability for the way the product was made, Wilson stated that some customers should not wear these pants as "they did not work on some women's bodies." Lululemon customers and the public were outraged by the statement.[14]

Wilson apologized in a video saying that he was sad and sorry. The company posted the video on Facebook and YouTube. However, there was intense uproar over his comments. Once again, blaming someone else (especially your customers) only makes a situation worse.[15] Wilson and Lululemon found this out quickly. Wilson later resigned from his role as Chairman of Board.

As an Ethical Marketer, it is important to recognize whether unethical behavior is a part of your company culture. Is this an isolated incident or does the blame game play out all the time? You need to identify if your company fosters a culture of blame, so you can move toward a culture of learning and fixing what is broken.

Unfortunately, if the blame game continues, then the problems will not be fixed, and you may risk severe future repercussions, not only with the media, but also with your customers.

Q55 What is the difference between misinformation and disinformation, and does it matter?

There is a big difference in the intent of the information and yes, it matters. Misinformation is what you share that you think is accurate and truthful. You do not realize what you are sharing or advocating for is something that is not verified, corroborated, truthful, or accurate in recount. You share because you believe it is true and you may "trust" the source that sent you the information.

Here is an example to demonstrate how easy it is to propagate misinformation. A video pops up on social media that has Dr. Anthony Fauci, MD from the National Institute of Health (NIH), saying the public does not have to wear masks. The video was created from an interview on March 8, 2020, before the CDC instructed the public to wear face coverings and to keep a distance of six feet from others.[16]

When groups who advocate for alternative medicines and are anti-vaccinations shared the video, the people watching did not know there was another CDC update on April 20th to wear face coverings. Many of these people did not look beyond the title of the video or understand the timing issue. Instead, they shared it widely in their social networks. As such, the video, due to the timing, became a part of a misinformation campaign. If Dr. Fauci was asked the same question in late April or May, his answer would have been different based on the severity of the pandemic in the US.

When it comes to disinformation, this is material or content with the intent to deliberately share the inaccurate and false information. Do you remember #Pizzagate? During the 2016 Presidential election, it was said that Hillary Clinton ran a pizza restaurant that was the front for a child sex-trafficking ring. There are no known proven and accurate sources behind the conspiracy, which was debunked, yet still shared by the media. According to Rolling Stone magazine, "We found ordinary people, online activists, bots, foreign agents and domestic political operatives" who were sharing the disinformation.[17]

When you share a debunked social media scandal you are participating in disinformation. It is this type of disinformation that led to a dangerous situation at the same DC pizza restaurant with a 28-year-old man from North Carolina. After seeing the news and believing what he read on social media about the abuse of children and the sex ring operation, he visited the pizzeria with an AR-15. He fired three rounds before he was arrested.

So, yes, it matters. Whether it is misinformation that is innocently spread or disinformation with pure negative intent, the onus is on the Ethical Marketer or the sharer. You have a choice and the where-with-all to make sure that information you share is supported, corroborated, accurate and helpful to all involved. At the same time, Ethical Marketers should be knowledgeable about the difference between misinformation and disinformation. You can also help to educate others on the importance of sticking with what is real, transparent, truthful and beneficial, especially when tensions are high and passion runs strong, such as the case in a Presidential election.

Q56 What happens if you do not know the answer to a media interview question?

Think of it this way ... you are in the doctor's office and she asks you a question. You do not know the answer, yet your health depends on it. Do you just make something up? Do you tell her something that is completely inaccurate? Do you give an answer because you want her to think you are really smart and not answering might make you look like less of a confident person? No ... you would not answer the question. You would say, "I'm not sure, however, this is what really bothers me ..."

Now, try to answer the question as it relates to media interviews. You are in a media interview and the journalist asks you a question outside of your knowledge base. Would you make up the answer? Would you share something that you are not supposed to or have no business sharing? Absolutely not. You are not going to conjure up an answer just for your own ego or to make yourself appear like you know everything. It is okay to respond in a manner that gives an appropriate answer based on who you are and what you do know.

For example, former CEO clients have asked me whether they should share information that is better suited for their CTOs or their Subject Matter Experts (SMEs). I advise them to say, "I don't have that information on hand, however, I'll connect you to ..." Or, they can say, "I'm happy to offer that information to you when I receive it." They can also say, "I'm not sure about this, however, what I can share is ..."

You do not always have to answer a question immediately, because, it is **not** okay to make up or give an answer that is **not** yours to share. This is why you will often hear healthcare experts, executives, scientists, politicians and others say, "I don't want to put words in anyone's mouth." Or, they say, "It's not for me to understand or speculate why [insert name] said ..."

Thought leaders who are Ethical Marketers should feel comfortable knowing they are expected to share what is transparent, accurate, truthful, helpful information, at the appropriate time, by their companies and the publics they serve. Sure, the media wants an answer. However, if you do not know, then it is your job to get them closer to the answer, which often means getting the information from somewhere else. These guidelines and ethical standards prevent professionals from answering a media question under pressure when they do not know and should not answer.

Q57 Can you trust the media to withhold your identity when you share information on background or "off the record?"

The answer lies in how well you know your media contact. Do you have a long-time relationship or is this a newer journalist or blogger you are working with for the first time? When it comes to sharing information on background or "off the record," you and your media friend must have the same definition of the terms.

The answer also comes down to trust. It is your agreement beforehand, which has to be spelled out. You can't assume that what you say during an interview, when it is not expressly spelled out as "on background" or "off the record," will stay out of an article or story.

For example, these two terms can mean the reporter will use the information in the story and just not attribute the information to you or your executive. The agreement can go as far as saying the reporter will not even hint at your identity by describing your position or the context of the information shared. Other reporters may agree that an on-background or off-the-record interview is information that will not be mentioned in the story. However, they use your information to corroborate information obtained from other sources.

Relationships are built on trust and trust takes time. It is unethical for a journalist, blogger or reporter to agree to keep something on background or off the record and then share your identity outright as the named source. Only with trust and an agreement beforehand can you share information on background and off the record. In all other cases, to be safe, consider everything "on the record."

Q58 Is it unethical if you want to be transparent, however, due to timing and circumstances, you are not allowed to share information with your constituents transparently?

Being transparent is a communication standard and it is appreciated by the audiences you serve. However, when there are circumstances that prevent you from sharing information for the protection, safety or well-being of others, then transparency has to wait. For these reasons, it is important to know when to hit the "pause button;" not to react too quickly. I remember a consulting session with a Sheriff's department in southern Florida when social media was fairly new to their police officers as a community building platform. When I was with the Sheriff and his officers, they were discussing the need to share and to be transparent with their community members. Yet, they realized quickly that the public on social media expected to receive information instantaneously, which brings a whole new meaning to breaking news, when you are an officer trying to do your job.

However, as officers who are at the scene of an incident first, they know to hit the pause button. Information should and can be shared after proper protocols are practiced. Unfortunately, social media creates transparency issues. For instance, when there is an accident, or a threatening situation, having photos at the scene show up on Facebook and Twitter may mean that people close to the incident or who have family or friends involved are being alerted in a way where the transparency hurts them, is not discreet and makes the situation far worse. So, as the appropriate procedures for contacting family members are going on through more traditional channels, social media does not abide by the "take a pause" rule. People in the community are seeing and sharing, which can be too much transparency too soon.

Ethical behavior means being transparent in a way that your information helps and is not harmful. Transparency is also an opportunity to build trust and credibility, which is needed especially when you are in law enforcement. Transparency should be constructive and reduce any wrongdoing. However, sharing information in haste, and that which is harmful to families or a larger community, causes pain and more damage. There is a time and a place to be transparent. Of course, in a tragic situation, you want to share the information with accuracy, no ambiguity, and with dignity and respect.

At the same time, transparency can also save lives. With the COVID-19 global pandemic, several Governors were sharing models or projections of the number of hospital beds (or lack thereof) and the shortage of Personal Protective Equipment (PPE) for the front-line responders in their states. They urged people to stay home even before there were stay home orders in place and businesses were shutting down due to the Coronavirus. The transparency in these Coronavirus press briefings was not always appreciated by the public. At times, there was frustration and disbelief. However, it was necessary to save lives, "flatten the curve" and stop the spread of the virus across the United States.

When it comes to transparency, here is a rule to follow … always share what will help and keep your community, organization, or company safe. Transparency comes with a responsibility and if done right, the trust will follow you, in your interviews or wherever you share.

The Marketing Experts "Weigh In" on Ethical Guidance

Media Interviews and Ethics Go Hand In Hand

By Winnie Sun, Founder of Sun Group Wealth Partners

I'm technically a financial advisor by trade. It will be almost 20 years, this year. In our industry especially, ethics and values are of the highest importance. As a financial advisor, I'm there to help, by giving our clients advice and guidance on their most important asset, which for many is the concentration of money they've saved up over the years. When you talk about financial planning in the news, ethics and values should be top of mind. We've seen the Bernie Madoffs of the world and different financial firms that have gone under. They have done things without keeping their client's best interest at heart or their ethics top of mind.

We have a responsibility: first as financial advisors to our clients; second, when we give interviews offering an audience insights, advice, and guidance on how they can make the most of their financial portfolio and to work toward financial independence. When interviewing, I believe we should live our lives the way that we tell it. I'm always really proud to talk with different reporters and they appreciate working with me. I share with them immediately, "The thing that you need to know is that I'm squeaky clean. I live a very clean life and my clients know where I stand." I also live in a way that they can be proud of when they invite me on their shows.

When it comes to the media, it's so easy to make a mistake. The value the media provides us is still huge, and it's such a responsibility for those of us who are the "talking heads." We need not only to provide value, but we also must understand the responsibility that we have. Every interview means embracing our values and presenting ourselves in such a way that our audience appreciates the information we're sharing. Then, looking back, our children and grandchildren will also feel proud to see the work we've done.

As an executive, it is exciting to get in front of the media. You're given the opportunity to talk about your business and what you do. However, you really have to sit back and realize you're under a microscope, from the moment you begin speaking until the end of the interview. Everything you say is going to be examined closely. You have to be really careful about the words and the extremes that you use. You want to deliver a message; however, it has to be compliant. Being sensitive, as you deliver messages, also means considering your goal. Is your goal just to go out there and talk about your company, or are you going out there with the intent to help people who are listening or watching you?

One of the advantages of being a financial adviser is that I plan everything. I think about extremes and I also think about how to phrase messages in a way that is going to help people. The last thing you want to do is have your message harm someone, cause someone to lose sleep, or to lose their money. Of course, the advice I give when interviewing with the media isn't always perfect. Yet, I try to give enough knowledge so that the person watching can say, "Okay, well that makes sense. I can see where she's going with this. I probably need to dig a little bit more, which means I might need to make an appointment with her, or someone else that's similar in her industry" The information you share should give someone enough to think about and also guide them to ask the right questions. As a financial advisor interviewing, I would not direct people on their finances, which is highly unethical. To advise is to know each person, and the particulars of a financial situation.

When I'm being interviewed by a media outlet, I've learned how important it is to "stick to your guns." For example, if someone is trying to pull information out of you, or a response isn't going to make you look your best, then you have to stick with what you know. When you're interviewing, you should assume you're not only speaking to your audience, but also speaking to a panel of attorneys. In my case, it could even be in regulatory or financial securities. Putting your best foot forward when you appear in the news means you're upholding your ethical duties to your clients, your firm and your industry.

Let Ethics Shine the Light to Guide You to True Freedom

By Stephanie Dalfonzo, Integrative Hypnotist, Coach and Author

I have been guided my entire life by honesty, fairness, equality, and diversity. In August 1992, I was working as DJ "Stevie Knox" on Y-100 (pop radio) in South Florida when Hurricane Andrew devastated parts of Dade County, near Miami. The radio station was in Ft. Lauderdale, about 40 miles north of the devastation. I suggested to Y-100's general manager that we hold a supply drive and we were overwhelmed with the response! We had a 100-vehicle caravan loaded with the desperately needed supplies. Unfortunately, at the National Guard checkpoint, we were refused access, saying the supplies needed to go through their system.

They did let the Y-100 van through and what I saw was horrifying—dead cows on the side of the road, devastation everywhere, people begging us for ice, batteries, milk for their babies and more. Since Y-100 was simulcasting the local TV station, my boss, in the van with me, suggested I call in with a report. As luck would have it, the head of the National Guard was live in the studio. I shared how our supply caravan was redirected, how desperately people needed them and ripped into the National Guard. I was cut off the broadcast and a few months later was fired for something else. (Coincidence?)

Twenty-eight years later, I would do it again (though with a bit less anger.) There is truth in the saying "How you do anything is how you do everything". You cannot be ethical in your personal life and not in your professional life and vice versa.

While my job was to entertain our listeners, I also regularly shined a light on various charitable organizations and endeavors. As a young wife and mother, that is who I was in my personal life and that is who I was in my professional life. Had I been ethical in my personal life, but not on air, the listeners would not have connected with me and come back to listen, day after day. I would like to think that by ethically pointing out how desperately Hurricane Andrew's victims needed the supplies, they got them in a timelier fashion.

My current career is as an Integrative Hypnotist, Coach, Speaker and Author of *Goodbye Anxiety, Hello Freedom*. My focus is to help people find their freedom—freedom from the past, freedom from failure and regrets, freedom from stress, anxiety, and fear. If I did not act out of a place of integrity, then I would not be able to help my clients act from their place of integrity and ethics—a place of true freedom.

Tell the Truth to Create Trust

By Suzanne Brown, Strategic Marketing and Business Consultant, Author

When dealing with the media, as PR professionals and marketers, our role is to influence and advocate for our brands or clients. We are helping tell a story about our brands and clients through a third party, which requires creating trust on many levels.

When it comes to presenting your brand, customers expect you to tell the truth and share the good and the bad. They want you to be vulnerable with the challenges you face instead of making everything appear picture perfect. They want the real story. It's what makes you more relatable and more of a brand that they can support.

The expectations of how you present your brand in the media are no different. Media professionals, viewers, and readers expect brands to have integrity as a fundamental pillar of their storytelling. Yes, they want to know it worked out and you have a good product or service. They don't want you to lie or sugar coat how it happened and what that experience looks like.

You might have heard the saying that any PR is good PR. The idea is that people are talking about you and that is enough. That is no longer the case. Bad PR gets your name on many people's lips, but it also often turns away potential and current customers.

Whether it's in a press conference, part of a news story, or even when you're quoted in an article, your audience, including your customers, holds you accountable for what you say and do. Your media contact expects the same. You must deliver on what you say. Your engagement with media requires your delivering on a promise, which is the backbone of having integrity in business.

So much of your engagement with the media is based on relationships (really, so much of marketing and PR is based on relationships). If you don't tell the truth about your product and service, or if you mislead a reporter with your quotes or feedback, intentionally provide misinformation about competitors, or show a lack of integrity, your relationships with the media are forever changed. You won't be someone the media seeks out. In fact, you'll probably be someone they avoid.

You need the media to trust you, whether you are a brand leader or a PR professional pitching that brand. Your relationships don't work without that trust. Period. And it's incredibly difficult to regain trust once its broken. It takes work and energy to establish and build these relationships.

They can be gone in an instant, though. This can dramatically impact how you do work for your brand or clients.

This also requires that leadership and the spokesperson for your business (e.g., a celebrity or influencer) truly reflect your brand's values. That requires choosing the right person to speak on behalf of your brand to the media. The person must live the values you want associated with your brand, especially integrity. When the people who speak on behalf of your brand stumble, your brand must deal with the repercussions, which can be a hard and painful experience.

Consider how many brands have had to right the course when a spokesperson has shown bad behavior or has misspoken. Ensuring you choose the right leadership and the right brand ambassadors helps. Keep in mind that it can also really help to get training for those who will be dealing with the media. Give your leadership team or spokesperson the right tools to fulfill their roles.

You must also understand that the media needs the public to trust what they're sharing as well. Just because a media outlet or journalist is willing to share your product or service or that of your client might not mean that you want to be associated with the journalist or the outlet. Be aware about where you're pitching, not just what you're pitching. Make sure that your brand is shown in the best light by being associated with high caliber outlets that are trusted in the marketplace and by current and potential customers.

Having integrity as part of how you run your business, whether for your brand or client, isn't always easy. There will be times when you're asked to cross the line into a grey area. That will reflect on you as a professional as much as it does on your brand or client. It's a personal choice to maintain integrity in your dealings with the media. And this integrity can help you, and the lack thereof can hurt you. Your reputation as a straight shooter can open doors, even from one media contact to another. Just as your negative and questionable interactions can quickly close those doors. You can make decisions or encourage choices that help build a brand known for its integrity.

Notes

1 Abigail Abrams, "'I Screwed Up': Sean Spicer Says He Regrets Comments on Inauguration Crowd Size and Hitler," Time, https://time.com/5088900/sean-spicer-screwed-up-inauguration-hitler, January 2018.

2 Bruce Weinstein, "Three Reasons Why White Lies Are The Worst Solutions to Your Problems," Forbes, https://www.forbes.com/sites/bruceweinstein/2018/02/28/three-reasons-why-white-lies-are-the-worst-solutions-to-your-problems/#37f051bf650e, February 2018.

3 Neil Garrett, Stephanie Lazzaro, Dan Ariely and Tali Sharot, "The brain adapts to dishonesty," Nature Neuroscience, https://www.nature.com/articles/nn.4426, October 2016.

4 Knowledge@Wharton, "When Do Exaggerations and Misstatements Cross the Line?" https://knowledge.wharton.upenn.edu/article/when-do-exaggerations-and-misstatements-cross-the-line, June 2010.

5 The Arthur W. Page Center, The Pillars of Public Relations Ethics, https://pagecentertraining.psu.edu/public-relations-ethics/core-ethical-principles/lesson-2-sample-title/the-pillars-of-public-relations-ethics, September 2020.

6 Remi Rosmarin, "A running list of brands giving back during the coronavirus pandemic," Insider, https://www.insider.com/brands-giving-back-during-the-coronavirus-pandemic, May 2020.

7 Corie Haylett, "21st Century Organizations and Newsjacking: Is this Ethical?", Corporate Compliance Insights, https://www.corporatecomplianceinsights.com/21st-century-organizations-and-newsjacking-is-this-ethical, July 2015.

8 Erica Ho, "Sandy Fail: American Apparel's Hurricane Sale Doesn't Go Over Well," Time, https://newsfeed.time.com/2012/10/31/a-little-bored-american-apparels-hurricane-sandy-sale-doesnt-go-over-well, October 2012.

9 Jessica Wohl, "J&J's latest headache caused by its o.b. tampons," Reuters, https://www.reuters.com/article/us-johnsonjohnson-tampons/jjs-latest-headache-caused-by-its-o-b-tampons-idUSTRE70I63P20110119, January 2011.

10 Airbnb, "We Accept," https://youtu.be/yetFk7QoSck, YouTube, February 2017.

11 Blake Morgan, "10 Powerful Examples of Corporate Apologies," Forbes, https://www.forbes.com/sites/blakemorgan/2018/10/24/10-powerful-examples-of-corporate-apologies/#1a1d28b940de, October 2018.

12 Danielle Douglas and Michael Fletcher, "Toyota reaches $1.2 billion settlement to end probe of accelerator problems," The Washington Post, https://www.washingtonpost.com/business/economy/toyota-reaches-12-billion-settlement-to-end-criminal-probe/2014/03/19/5738a3c4-af69-11e3-9627-c65021d6d572_story.html, March 2014.

13 Matt Daily, "BP, other oil spill companies start the blame game," Reuters, https://www.reuters.com/article/us-oil-rig-blame/bp-other-oil-spill-companies-start-the-blame-game-idUSTRE64578H20100506, May 2010.

14 Alex Honeysett, "They Said What? 3 CEO Media Blunders We Can Learn From," The Muse, https://www.themuse.com/advice/they-said-what-3-ceo-media-blunders-we-can-learn-from, November 2013.

15 CBSNews, "Lululemon founder Chip Wilson issues apology following thigh-rubbing pants comments," https://www.cbsnews.com/news/lululemon-founder-chip-wilson-issues-apology-following-thigh-rubbing-pants-comments, November 2013.

16 Saranac Hale Spencer, "Outdated Fauci Video on Masks Shared Out of Context," FactCheck, https://www.factcheck.org/2020/05/outdated-fauci-video-on-face-masks-shared-out-of-context, May 2020.

17 Amanda Robb, "Anatomy of a Fake News Scandal," Rolling Stone, https://medium.com/rollingstone/anatomy-of-a-fake-news-scandal-d5494e2837c3, November 2017.

Chapter 5

Filtering Ethics Through Your Organization

Do you think an organization has a conscience? This is a heavily debated question. For the purpose of this book, let's say the organization does not have one. However, the people who make up the organization all do, and they form the "collective conscience." They are responsible for upholding the company values and ethical standards through all of their interactions and through every communications channel. However, a couple of challenging questions remain. First, where does the collective conscience begin? Second, how does an army of ethical champions (all of the employees) follow through with good judgment and ethical standards daily?

Because ethics and values show up prominently in communication, take a look at three key areas of the organization with the resources and responsibility to drive ethics and values: the communications department, the C-Suite or leadership team and the HR department. All three parts have to be connected. Granted, one can argue that social media does have communication flowing in and out of all different departments, often unchecked. However, there are checks and balances and best practices companies can set up through communications, leadership, and HR to help filter ethics through the rest of the organization.

We have already determined in Chapter 2 that the marketing and PR professionals in your communications department are given the unofficial title of the "Ethical Marketers." They report to their leaders which include the top levels of a firm. These leaders are also considered Ethical Marketers or role models. We will address leaders as ethical role models in more depth in Chapter 7, as they have a megaphone to share organizational policy and official communications.

At the same time, HR serves the function as Ethical Marketers, making sure ethics is handled as a company policy, working to standardize a Code of Conduct for all employees, whether the guidelines appear during an onboarding process, in a hardcopy signed handbook, online with ethics training, or wherever they live for employees to access and learn. Most importantly when the three groups are working cohesively, ethics and values become more than words on a "page" and go beyond an online test to benchmark behavior with a score. Instead, they become the shared beliefs driving the collective conscience with ethical behavior, from employee minds to their hearts to the subsequent communications and interactions that ensue.

When you filter ethics through an organization you are focused on the importance of building ethical champions throughout your company. You can begin with the PR people, marketers, and your communications department; look to the company leaders for role modeling behavior; and package the ethics and values through HR to penetrate the collective conscience through policies. With all three parts working, ethics will permeate every level and rank in your company, with your people who "walk" the "ethics talk." You are moving from "we have core values" to "we are a company that believes, practices and stands by our ethics, values and good judgment."

Whether you are a young professional or a seasoned veteran, you are aligning yourself with your company's ethics and values. You, as a part of a collective conscience, are judged regardless the size, the industry or the figure that is attached to your bottom-line. Practicing ethics, at every touchpoint, means working diligently on your internal communication as a great starting point. After all, company employees are the gateway to your customers and other important stakeholders.

Q59 Where does ethics begin in a company, with its leaders or with the communications department?

In an ideal situation, ethics can start with the founders and leaders who form the organization. Then, as a best-case scenario, the communications department and HR department build those ethics and values into the company culture and through their communication programs. However, when entrepreneurs start out and their companies are scaling quickly, although they may have their own set of ethics and values, they do not always materialize until later in the company's growth timeline.

I remember working with a 200-person tech company that was making a series of acquisitions to grow quickly. As companies expand in size and numbers, they are merging processes, technology, and people. As you can imagine, it is an exciting time to increase infrastructure, service offerings and expand into different markets. It is also a time of blending cultures and people are looking toward leadership for company direction, mission, vision, and, yes, values. However, as the HR area condensed, it was apparent that despite 10 years of business there was no clear path to ethics and values spelled out for the company employees. At a time when social media was being adopted by departments across the organization, and now in different regions of the world, it also became evident that not only did they need to spell out the ethics and values, but these values also had to go across all of their channels.

The example is not atypical. There are companies that grow quickly, and it is not until a growth tipping point that they realize they need to back track in the policy arena. At the same time, there are the instances of crisis that also send companies scrambling to develop and crystalize their values and ethical conduct through all their interactions and communications channels. Of course, this is the worst-case scenario and one, in hindsight, which has leaders, and communications and HR professionals realizing that the road to ethics and values should start early on, with education to prevent missteps and unethical behavior.

The answer ... share beliefs and values early on and talk about ethical conduct. Ethics can start in any of three places mentioned previously. As an Ethical Marketer, you should strive to make sure values take shape in your culture before an unpleasant situation forces policy rather than it being there to guide employees in the first place.

Q60 Why does unethical communication matter to people who are not in the communications department?

The answer requires another simple question ... why does reputation matter to the people who are not in the PR or communications department? It is the exact same reason. Companies need a good reputation to thrive and flourish in the market. When your cup of "goodwill" is full, your customers, shareholders, employees, partners, suppliers, media, etc., all benefit from your good reputation. When your standing is challenged and a bad reputation leads to brand damage, and cuts your bottom line, everyone tied to the company gets hurt.

Now, back to the ethics question. When unethical communication makes its way out to the public, it may seem as if it is a leadership problem or it is a brand issue. However, unethical behavior also directly affects how your people feel about the company leaders. When employees learn about questionable behavior, their immediate reaction may be disbelief. Then, if the accusations about the unethical behavior become more apparent, they move to disappointment and upset over the lack of transparency or the way they find out, possibly from the media, their own customers, or through social media. Of course, the communications transparency should come from their own leaders.

Then, depending on the severity of the offense and the steps taken to rectify the situation, there is the issue of trust. It can take many years to build trust and it only takes a short time to break that same bond. Here is what happens when trust breaks down with employees:

- There is a weakening of the employee collaboration and the sense of community with the company leadership.

- Public credibility issues and the negative reputation backlash can affect employee productivity and overall company moral.
- Loss of customers due to ethical missteps can result in a lack of employee motivation and the subsequent loss of trust, which, in turn, may lead to a mass employee exodus.

Of course, not every communications misstep or a decision made with poor judgment will lead to mass exodus. However, the breakdown of community, collaboration, productivity, and motivation are not just a communications department, HR or leadership issue. The impact goes far beyond the any one particular area, affecting all employees in a company.

Ethical communication, wherever it originates and regardless of who does the actual sharing of the communication, matters to everyone who has a relationship with the company.

Q61 What is the best way to find out about ethics for an organization?

Although you would expect employees to find out about ethics during their employment onboarding process, learning about ethics should be an ongoing process. Most employees come into the organization looking for information; curious about the culture and how to best fit into their new environment. The company handbook usually gives a good overview of organizational values and ethical behavior and so does a company's website. They learn early on the dos and the don'ts of ethics, which are spelled out in writing, and often a signature is required to show an understanding of the ethics policy or Code of Conduct. However, finding out about ethics in this manner is static and does not necessarily allow an employee to see how values and good judgment need to play out in different scenarios.

Your HR department should serve as the educator and the disseminator of ethical standards (a Code of Conduct) by developing policies and ethics training at different intervals, at the very least as an annual online training course. Timing wise, it would take less than an hour to prove that you have read, been tested and understood an updated version. However, when incidents happen within your company or even publicly, many companies will take it upon themselves to add in additional communication to help employees understand how to handle more specific challenges they face.

For instance, during the racial tensions and protests due to the death of George Floyd in Minneapolis, Minnesota, companies had their leadership speak out about racial violence to employees in their firms. Their statements were both in private and in public. Virtual Town Hall meetings were an effective way to reach employees in a timely matter.

At times of issue and crisis, employees may seek advice from company officials. During the Town Hall meetings they can ask questions regarding conduct or acceptable behavior. If the executives are unable to answer all of the questions, as in the case of a large global company, the questions not answered become available for all employees in the form of an FAQ around the ethical conduct in question.

There will always be new ways that employees will want to receive information about company policies and how it will affect their roles and responsibilities. However, from a communications standpoint, if you are in the PR or marketing department, the best way to find out is to be proactive and to ask. What is not spelled out falls within your realm; for you to question and to help provide the answers.

If the tools, information and training are not in place, no matter your position, title or rank, then the best answer to this question is to simply ask. Be proactive about ethics. Your proactiveness will show not only in your interactions and your relationships internally, but also with your customers and different groups publicly.

Q62 What are some of the common problems in organizations where ethical issues can occur?

Is it a problematic area of the company or the people who make up the area that cause the problems? In other words, one might suspect that marketing and sales are areas with common problems. Both areas work together to drive leads and sales. When there are numbers and quotas to be achieved, does the ethical conduct and compliance suffer? For the purpose of this argument, because an area does not have an ethical conscience, similar to the debate about organizations, perhaps a breakdown of unethical practices by professionals in different areas of the company is the best way to identify the problem "hot spots."

Staying with the same example, the sales and marketing departments, it is easier to identify some of the behaviors that may cause issues for the company, both internally and externally. Here are some behaviors to watch; behaviors that can also be applied to other areas too:

- **Misrepresenting the numbers.** For this unethical practice, marketing and sales can be a hot bed of issues, with the pressures to overperform, exceed values, and to show every dollar invested has a return on investment. Manipulating the numbers can often stem from the pressures to perform depending on how much the numbers reflect compensation and/or yearly bonuses.
- **Discrimination, harassment, and racism in communications.** Whether intentional or not, harmful statements, actions, and interactions through social media or other media channels can cause hurt and public harm. Take a look at Quaker Oats' long-time brand, Aunt Jemima Syrup. Today, with racial protests after the killing of George

Floyd and other brutality cases against Black Americans, the company has acknowledged their logo, which is more than 130 years old, will be retired because the origins are "based on a racial stereotype."[1]

- **Technology and data privacy.** Marketing and sales are interested in finding the most targeted ways to reach and convince customers to purchase products and services. It is the personalized experience that delights a customer and provides rich data intelligence. Yet, it is also the lack of transparency in the collection process that can cause issues with the public.

- **Lying to customers and/or misrepresenting services.** When Dannon launched their Activia brand of yogurt, it was marketed as "clinically" and "scientifically" able to boost a person's immune system. As a result, Activia was also sold at a higher price than other competitive brands. It was not until a $45 million lawsuit was filed and a judge deemed these claims were unproven that Dannon removed the specific wording from its product packaging.[2]

- **Confidentiality with competitive information.** Companies use competitive intelligence as a way to develop their value propositions and their positioning statements prior to a go-to-market launch. However, it is the unethical collection of certain types of proprietary materials that causes ethical concern. For example, obtaining sensitive material a competitor has worked diligently to protect or using unethical practices to get this information, are also an issue falling within the marketing and sales departments.

These are several of the well-known issues. Other problems may include bribery, fairness in business practices, deferential pricing and the list goes on. However, if you look at the list, it is not isolated to sales and marketing. The unethical behaviors can move across an organization and infiltrate any area. Therefore, it takes an army of ethical champions to become aware and get educated on identifying and acting to prevent any hot spots from bubbling up.

If you can catch the potential problem before it bubbles up, then it is also less likely to branch out to other areas inside your organization.

Q63 Is it ever right to share information externally that is frowned upon by your organization?

If you are taking more than a few seconds to answer this question then you might be in the wrong organization or feeling misaligned with your values. There is a difference between information, which is not yours to share through your personal channels (for example, proprietary or sensitive material information that belongs to the company) vs. the kind of communication the company executives deem "inappropriate" and they frown upon.

Is what you would like to share incongruent with what the company deems sharable? Here is the point in time that you have to test your values. If you know that information is true, fair, accurate and helpful to customers and not breaking any confidentiality agreements or laws, then you would want to share it. If you have opinions that are expressly of your own account and knowledge, then you would say them. A company should not control what you say or do for its own political agenda or that of its customers. When you are told the company "frowns" on this type of information, or they discourage you from "saying this or that" because it is not what customers like or agree with, then plainly and simply, it may be time to move on to your next position.

If you feel the need to share and you are inspired by the communication and your company views the opposite, then you are out of alignment with your firm. Let the company "frown" as much as it wants. In turn, you will smile when you are working for another company that is more aligned with who you are and who is onboard with what you believe.

Q64 Who in the company can help you to make better ethical decisions?

First take a look at who is closest to you for initial ethics guidance. For instance, your mentor or sponsor within your company will help you. It is their business acumen at the firm, as well as their experience in the area of ethics, that is there to guide you. You can also look to areas of your company that are set up to help you navigate ethical decisions and tough challenges you are facing.

As an Ethical Marketer, your company may have these resources, or they need to be developed for all of your ethical champions:

- **Talent Office.** In larger organizations, the Talent Office can be one of three areas in the HR department. Talent is the area that is known to attract, onboard, motivate and retain high-performing employees. As a part of the HR responsibilities to develop employees, the Talent Office creates and promotes an environment for ethical conduct that is fair and just for all company employees.
- **Policy Repository.** In order to practice company values and uphold ethical standards, companies offer employees a repository to access, download, and review all company policies including their ethical code of conduct. Even though there is a designated area to find materials, most companies will update employees via email, push notifications, and through internal communications channels about any policy updates.

- **Risk Management.** The Risk Management area is tasked with financial forecasting and evaluating company risk in business and is tied closely to company ethics. After all, if you practice good risk management then you are, indeed, practicing good ethics. The two go hand-in-hand in a business. Often Risk Management is a resource to help people navigate risks and to make better business decisions for the company.[3]
- **Legal Department.** When you go to your legal department then you *know* there is a serious ethical issue or unethical conduct is playing out more widespread at your company. However, it is important to remember that you can have an unethical issue that is legal. Remember, getting advice from legal also comes from a "legal" frame of reference knowing that your company is the client rather than any public group, if the issue is outward facing.
- **Ethics Hotline.** An ethics Code of Conduct is not just an internal resource. A hotline can be an ethical resource used for employees, clients, partners, and any interested party doing business with a firm. Most hotlines allow professionals to anonymously file a claim online or ask a question regarding the organization's Code of Conduct. Companies may advise their constituents that the hotline should be used after other channels have been explored and not as a go-to resource.
- **Ethics Advisors/Ethics Oversight Board.** Companies often establish an ethics committee or board that has oversite of their business ethical conduct. For example, EY in the United States has an Ethical Oversight Committee set up by US executives helping to promote uniformity and best practices with respect to their organization's values and Code of Ethical Conduct.[4]

Whether your organization has one or all of these resources, the more opportunities to support ethical communication and interactions aligned with company policy the better. It is the shared beliefs and standards with adequate tools and resources that help employees, or any group, to make better decisions and to undertake ethical actions in challenging situations.

Q65 What is the intersection between ethics in PR, marketing, sales, and customer service?

The intersection is in the communication and the Customer Experience (CX). Today CX may seem like an overused term. However, your CX is at the heart of your business and it is what differentiates you from any other product or service. Customers are loyal to the brands that take into consideration a sum total of their experiences through every different company touchpoint. Public relations, marketing, sales, and customer service can make up the bulk of the planned, as well as the unplanned, conversations.

When PR, marketing, sales, and customer service are aligned, your customer is provided the best experience, free of some of the issues that arise when there is a disconnect. For example, these areas can have checks and balances when it comes to the four Ps in marketing:

- **Product.** When companies develop products, they keep their customers in mind. For example, the development of products that are good quality and are safe to use. Customers expect to experience products that satisfy their needs. Of course, if this is not the case, these areas will rally to identify all of the communication, conversations, and information from a dissatisfied customer.

- **Promotion.** What the product does, and the real benefits, are how it should be promoted. These areas are all tied together from the information that is created and promoted (truthful vs. deceptive) to how customers share about their experience. If they have a less than satisfactory encounter or experience something they feel is not in their best interest, then customer service will be among the first to hear about the issue.

- **Price.** Setting the price should be consistent and fair to all customers. Marketers will set the price and from awareness to purchase these areas are all responsible to the customer when questions arise or conversations around pricing concerns occur. The internal sharing of pricing information and the pricing itself reflect an existing cost structure. If pricing should be an issue, along with marketing, sales and customer service, then PR must be alerted to respond to public inquiries or backlash.

- **Place.** With so many touchpoints today, customers are receiving information from all different places. For this reason, being sure not to manipulate customers through different channels is especially important. Sales, marketing, and PR know there are vulnerable populations, whether it is targeting children, minorities or undereducated groups. Because sales, marketing, PR, and customer service are among the areas with the highest communication, and promotional touchpoints, these areas must collaborate and align in terms of the standards of material distribution.

The company silos broke down a long time ago. Ethical Marketers realize the intersection and alignment between PR, marketing, sales, and customer service are the point at which customer experience has the potential to reach its highest marks. The intersection between these areas is the point where customers' needs, wants, and expectations from their favorite brands are exceeded.

Q66 What can you do to prevent poor judgment in communications?

Whether it is good judgment or poor reasoning that plays out, it is someone's choice. Was that choice made alone? Were there any open discussions within marketing, PR, or with senior leaders to add an outside perspective. Fostering an environment of trust and communication, without judgment or fear of repercussions, is the first step to preventing unnecessary missteps from occurring. When there is trust between team members it is much easier to share the "red flags" or the communication concerns before mistakes are made.

The question becomes how do you build the kind of trust with your team to create a more open dialog that promotes varying perspectives? Trust is built over time and comes from vulnerability and transparency. Knowing every member of your team is human and has a life outside of work is important information. If you want to build trust among your team members then this means putting aside some time to learn more about one another outside of work, and to have resources and activities ready to help.

When I taught for the Fairleigh Dickinson University Global Business Management (GBM) program, one of the courses was a Sophomore Business Forum class. We used team building to help the student groups learn more about each other. The goal was to have students feel comfortable and work more productively, and in harmony, on their final semester projects. There are any number of exercises you can use to get people to connect and to build trust on teams. Here are two exercises that I used, all easy activities, which lead to instant engagement and trust over time.

Trust Building Activity #1: Try some back-to-back drawing. This exercise has your team broken into groups of two. Each pair sits back-to-back in their chairs. You give each person on the team a unique drawing; either a combination of shapes that are touching, or an obscure object. One member, at a time, will describe his or her shape to the other team member to draw through voice command only, not being able to see the actual shape the teammate is describing. Teams of two complete the exercise and switch, so the person who was drawing is now describing a different shape to his or her teammate to draw based on what is shared.

Once the second drawing is complete, make a comparison. How did the hand-drawn pictures look against the actual photo of the shapes? Were the pictures drawn by the pair accurate, based on listening to the directions on how to draw the shapes? Sometimes a team will rotate partners to see how different pairs work together. The goal is to have pictures drawn which are close to the photos described. When you can draw based on voice instructions it shows how a team listens, visualizes and takes instruction well. The drawing likeness increases when trust exists between teammates.

Trust Building Activity #2: Time for the one-question icebreaker. Here is the easiest and least awkward team building exercise, which gets your team on the road to trust by learning something a little more personal. If you have a small team then you can have the entire team answer a simple ice-breaker question before your meeting starts. Examples of questions can be:

- What is your favorite movie and why?
- What is one thing the team does not know about you?
- What is your favorite meal?
- If you could meet any person (alive or dead), who would it be and why?

If you have more than six people on your team, then you should take some time to pair off into groups of two or three. Have each person in the group answer an icebreaker question to learn more. You will want to mix up your groups of three or four at the start of meetings so people can learn new insights about the different team members.

If you take the time to have team members get to know one another better, the dialogue becomes more open and authentic, and less judgmental. With more ease of sharing, fewer mistakes and ethical missteps will occur as people begin to trust and open up about what they are seeing and experiencing, and if they have concerns regarding any company communications.

Q67 What should you do if your colleague or higher-up is communicating and exercising poor judgment?

Years ago, the answer was simple. You would go directly to the person to consult with those colleagues by asking questions, sharing thoughts, and helping them to possibly see a different perspective. Conversations would focus on each team members ability to avoid compromising integrity, upholding company values, and also treating others with respect, at all times. These discussions were taking place behind the scenes in many departments, not just communications.

Having an open door to discuss issues in a "safe" environment where people felt comfortable and did not feel judged was also really helpful. Today, organizational climates have changed. With an uptick in company issues regarding diversity, equity, inclusion and racism and the nature of internal communication that surely spreads externally more quickly through social media, other company protocols must be in place. For example, today, it is not enough to just confront your colleague; there are more action steps to ensure that any poor judgment does not play out and that ethical standards and protocol are not broken.

All employees, from every department, should be encouraged to act with three steps. The first is to share thoughts directly with the person with whom you have the concern. The next step involves your direct supervisor, who can also help to add a different perspective and reinforce good judgment in decision-making. Lastly, any incidents that have played out which challenge the company's values and ethical standards have to be documented by the HR department.

Companies will usually spell out their action steps for handling these types of situations. Larger companies may have additional steps, as their resources to uphold an ethical code of conduct are vast. The key to handling any colleague who is exhibiting poor judgment is to be educated on good judgment and to have an organization reinforcing those values and ethics. The goal is to use checks and balances and education so that every employee action helps and is not damaging the company and the people it serves, including you as the Ethical Marketer.

Q68 Should companies require ethical testing for all employees or just employees who handle communication?

Ethical testing is not only for the people who are the official communicators of a company. Today, the customer touchpoints go far beyond the areas that are the most known to be the gateways to contact with customers. Every area of the company and each professional title has the ability to share about the company and to connect with the company's constituents in myriad places. Social media also makes it possible for everyone to create content, collaborate globally and share with groups connected to the organization in different regions, with no official communications, customer service or sales titles necessary.

For this reason, ethical testing has to be done annually, at the very least, or at times when the company's values or ethical standards have been questioned. However, taking a test is clearly not enough. It is important for managers and directors to have conversations with their teams so that employees can ask question of their supervisors or know that they can bring their ethical questions and concerns to other resources or areas set up within the organization.

Organizations benefit when employees engage in testing. An ethical testing program helps professionals to learn about the different situations where communication and their actions have the opportunity to uphold the values of the company internally with peers, as well as with any company stakeholder. From customers and partners to media, analysts and shareholders, ethics testing shows in the interactions with these groups.

When ethics are a part of the company culture, then testing also becomes a natural method relied upon for updating knowledge and skills in the organization.

Q69 How do you build ethical champions in your company?

Modelling ethical behavior, at the upper echelons of the company, helps to build ethical champions. Although Chapter 7 covers ethical executive role models in detail, it is important to mention that all employees should be ethical role models, not just company leadership. You can be a role model at any level, and this is a personal choice. When more employees realize the values they hold personally match that of their company, ethical behavior becomes both a personal choice and a business practice.

Many companies are recognizing employees who show sound judgment and who exercise good conduct and uphold values. For example, companies will reward employees faced with challenges who demonstrate ethical behavior by:

- Offering a profit-sharing system where employees are receiving a portion of the company profits quarter or annually. When ethics are upheld it is a win-win for everyone.
- Promoting the employees who are the outstanding ethical champions and who clearly serve as the role models for good judgment in decision-making and in their communication.
- Setting up a rewards system, which could be anything from financial bonuses to additional vacation days or comp or compensatory time.

Most companies will invest in these programs as they realize the largest reward for ethical behavior and good judgment in decision-making. They understand the reward of the loyal customer who trusts the company and its employees. These customers want to do business repeatedly with a brand that conducts itself ethically through all communications and actions in the market.

The Marketing Experts "Weigh In" on Ethical Guidance

Ethical Obligations to Society and Ourselves

By Tess Kossow, Author and Entrepreneur

Ethics.

It's deeper than deciding what is right and what is wrong. Most people can do that.

Ethics goes beyond the brain's ability to make a decision and then balance that decision with whether or not that choice is what's truly best for the situation at hand, taking in the emotional consideration of all details. It deals with our morals and our individual obligations to society and quite frankly, to ourselves. And more specifically, ethics are often referred to as an activity or topic of discussion rather than a general platform.

In my professional life, I have dealt with ethically challenging situations that have given me nightmares. Hirings that needed to comply with racial and age demographics vs. the best qualifications needed for the job. Firings that looked beyond job eliminations into future company quotas that needed to be exceeded, even if the company was barely staying afloat with the staff at hand. And in those situations, I often asked myself, is this ethically correct? Am I going a certain direction because the boss said so or because it's what the client needs or because it's the right thing to do? Being paid under-the-table to hold a certain seat available for a client in an establishment, when others might want to sit there, because this particular client comes in and spends a lot of money. Or how about allowing an employee not to participate in preparing certain reports because they contribute in other essential ways, when everyone else has to follow protocol?

Don't ask questions; just follow along if you want to keep your job. After all, it benefits the company, and I have bills to pay …

But our ethics and ethical decisions don't stop with a paycheck. From the moment we wake, until the moment we fall asleep, ethics are constantly thrown in our face.

When I left corporate America to start my own company, I made the decision to walk away from my current position after a number of moments happened in which I realized that it was the only way to make a statement. I stood alone in my thoughts and yet, I had never felt so empowered with a rush of intuition to do what I knew was right for my life.

On the flip side, I realized that there was no more guidance telling me what I needed to do in a situation; now that I was on my own.

Take, for example, my first children's picture book. I reference "genetic testing" in easy to rhyme words that correspond with beautiful pictures. I write from the heart and from personal experience. That's how I find connection to what I produce in the market.

However, many people do not agree with my decision to have done genetic testing on my embryos when I was going through IVF. I had to thaw and discard one embryo because it came back from genetic testing abnormal with either missing or extra chromosomes. Discarding this embryo had nothing to do with selfish desires on how the baby would turn out or some kind of attempt to "pick and choose" the perfect child for me. It had nothing to do with me "playing God," as I have heard before. This decision to have genetic testing performed on my embryos had everything to do with the medical staff wanting to protect my health and prepare the best situation for a healthy, positive pregnancy without putting my well-being in danger, which would ultimately put the baby in danger.

Ironically, after a miscarriage with a healthy embryo that was transferred, I had another ethical decision to make when the last embryo I had came back from genetic testing failing to yield results and recommending it be re-biopsied. I could have donated that embryo to science or to another family looking to conceive without genetic testing. I could have discarded that embryo and went another direction to motherhood. I chose to retest that embryo that originally failed amplification, and it turned out to be a normal embryo suitable for transfer.

I transferred that embryo within me.

That embryo today is my son.

When I stop to think about the "what ifs" from those life changing decisions I made, I often lose my breath. Any other way I could have gone might have made or broken the opportunity for me to become a mama. And yet, ethically, none of the decisions were wrong.

However, all but one wasn't right for me.

And so, mentioning genetic testing in *I'mVeryFerris, a child's story about in vitro fertilizatio*n is non-negotiable. It touched on my morals, my complete mindset in how I now view the meaning of life, and how I want others to understand and respect all the intricate details that go into IVF.

So many of our decisions can really make us stop and pivot in a new direction. And that also goes for the negative of not making any decisions and falling into a pattern where nothing happens. This ultimately keeps us from experiencing opportunities and moments that could have positive impacts on our mental and physical health.

Because ethics don't stop at the door.

They are literally challenging us to choose if our decisions will be for the better of the moment at hand all the while good for us and how we live our lives.

It's not easy, is it?

But, when I look at my life and my baby and my business, popular or not, I did what was morally right for me and live every day knowing that with all the facts in front of me, I made the best decision I could, which has gotten me to this moment in time.

Can you say the same with what you are about to do?

Steering Toward the Ethical Organization

By Suzanne Brown, Strategic Marketing and Business Consultant, Author

I define the three most important qualities in a leader as having vision, resilience, and integrity. You want a leader with a unique idea and perspective. And you want a leader who can quickly bounce back from challenges and failure.

But winning at any cost isn't leadership; it's a lack of leadership. Leaders must build their business, based on trust, the backbone of any client relationship. Trust is the foundation of a brand and what it stands for. You're giving your word—risking your reputation again and again—with the end result of delivering what and when you say you'll deliver.

Integrity isn't seasonal. You don't only have integrity when things are going well and do what you have to when things get tough. It's not a matter of having some integrity. And you're not only ethical when others are watching. You either have integrity or you do not.

Growing up, my dad often talked about the importance of your word. A word and handshake are enough (but you still want to get it all in a contract). You mean what you say and you follow through and deliver. This is the foundation of integrity in business and life.

I'm not unique in getting that first glimpse of integrity from my parents and family. As children, we watch and mimic what we see. And then we see how our classmates deal with challenging ethical moments. How does someone else deal with the class bully when he/she is picking on someone else? Does a friend cheat on a test and get a good grade but you don't, even though you studied harder? We observe how behaviors and repercussions match up and start to take notice.

We rarely formally teach integrity in the typical K-12 school environment. Your school might have you sign an honor code at some point, but do we even really understand what that means at that age? We're often not coached on this, outside of family input. And, let's face it, not all families are focusing on teaching kids ethical behavior.

Depending on your university program, you might have taken an ethics class as an undergraduate or even a graduate student. I went to graduate school shortly after several companies' complete lack of ethics was put under a microscope—companies such as Enron, WorldCom, and Arthur Andersen. Each of these companies' questionable business decisions and corporate greed led to bankruptcy. And those business practices led to new federal laws and processes required by the Securities and Exchange Commission.

As a result of this unethical behavior, we started a new conversation about ethics and business. In fact, the then-dean of the MBA program that I attended taught the ethics class. There were many lively debates about the people working for companies like the Enrons of the world and how they allowed unethical behavior to happen.

Interestingly, there were a few MBA students in the class who had been at Enron just before grad school. And they were very honest in saying they didn't know about the unethical behavior. They were smart, engaged employees, but they simply weren't privy to those unethical decisions and didn't have access to that information. They thought they had joined a top company in their industry.

So, the question becomes, who is the source of ethics at a company. Is it senior leadership or HR? Is it the marketing team that owns the branding? No and yes. It's not *only* the senior leadership team, marketing, or HR. It must come from all levels and departments and be in the company DNA and a basic part of how the company does business daily.

Many junior marketers learn by observing their leaders. So, we hope that managers and senior leaders show integrity. We need to talk about these topics with potential employees and then with new hires, especially in key areas like marketing. As a company, how do you expect employees, clients, and suppliers to behave? If someone is racist or takes advantage of those of the opposite sex but who is a top seller, is that acceptable? Do you mistreat your marketing agency team but still get results? We must have open, honest conversations to ensure unethical behavior is unacceptable. What if we showed employees, through case studies (especially of things that went wrong) and role play, how to choose ethical behavior?

As a marketer, I've had the good fortune of working for employers and clients whose values aligned with mine. I was comfortable with the decisions being made by leaders because I would have made similar decisions in their place. The only time my values didn't align, I left within six months of joining the company. Finding these ethical companies within the marketing industry wasn't hard. I sought out those employers. I did my homework to understand their reputation. I asked questions during the interview process. I noticed the language employees used and avoided.

I'll leave you with this final thought. We each have our code of ethics. Each company has its own version of ethical behavior. As a marketer, align yourself with people and businesses that uphold your values. Any company or individual that asks you to bend your code of ethics is not worth your time and energy. Even if it's a well-known resume-building opportunity, it's not worth it. There will be other opportunities down the road that align with your ethics that allow you to learn new skills and grow.

Notes

1 Jordan Valinsky, "The Aunt Jemimah brand, acknowledging its racist past, will be retired," CNN Business, https://www.cnn.com/2020/06/17/business/aunt-jem ima-logo-change/index.html, June 2020.
2 Will Heilpern, "18 false advertising scandals that cost some brands millions," Business Insider, https://www.businessinsider.com/false-advertising-scandals-2016 -3#activia-yogurt-said-it-had-special-bacterial-ingredients-2, March 2016.
3 IRMI, Expert Commentary, "Why Link Risk Management and Ethics," https://www.irmi.com/articles/expert-commentary/why-link-risk-management-and-ethics #, February 2005.
4 EY, Global Code of Conduct, https://assets.ey.com/content/dam/ey-sites/ey-com/ en_gl/home-index/ey-global-code-of-conduct-english.pdf, pg. 19, April 2020.

Chapter 6

Learning Ethics from a Mentor

Mentors are all around you. They can be colleagues at your company, peers in your social media communities, or the members of your professional associations. However, finding the right mentor means asking the qualifying questions, knowing this professional is invested in your growth, and you have the right alignment; all with a goal to further develop your knowledge and skills. Questions you might ask, as you screen your mentors, may focus on common purpose, level of commitment, experience in an industry and challenges they have faced. Finding the right alignment shows in the strength of the relationship with your mentor over time.

When you find a good mentor, it is someone who you can trust and whose advice you value. At the same time, whether you realize it or not, you are also looking for this person to be an ethical mentor. This is your role model who is willing to share stories and personal situations and how he or she has applied ethics and values to every situation. Your mentor should represent the epitome of ethics, as demonstrated through intentions, aspirations, interactions, and communication that spans a career and a lifetime.

When I was in college, and later in my MBA program, I did not think about selecting mentors, based on their ethical conduct. Not that it wasn't important. Inherently, I thought it was baked into to the professional's DNA. I automatically thought it came with the territory. I did not feel as if I had to ask, "What are your values and are you ethical in all of your communications and business transactions?" Maybe these are questions that need to be asked today. You can be the judge of this approach.

However, what I did realize was that after finding and building a relationship with my mentors, their ethics and values came through their insights and advice. Thankfully, it was a natural part of who they were, and how they conducted themselves personally and professionally.

Of course, when you are a part of the PR industry, like me, ethical role models surround you. There is no shortage of leaders who pride themselves on ethical communication and they are ready to impart sound advice. Like all mentors, whether it is PR, marketing or the profession of your choice, mentors are happy to share the good, the bad and the ugly of their ethics education in business. You can also rely on a mentor to give you a subtle reminder; why it is important to take ethics seriously and with great pride. Because mentors are chosen carefully and with trust, your mentor will be the first one to let you know if and why a decision you have made is a good one, or not. Better yet, they can guide you before making any missteps.

Because we all need ethical mentors, the mentors selected for this chapter are weighing in on their principles and ethical decision-making processes. They are answering the frequently asked questions while they share their approach with you. In this chapter, learning ethics from a mentor is an opportunity for you to have more mentors to guide you. These thought leaders, from various industries, and with different experiences, share answers to questions that offer deep insights, direction, and a path for you to reinforce your values and make ethical decisions too.

Q70 How can learning ethics by example occur?

By Susan Freeman, CEO, Freeman Means Business and founder of the Executive Institute on Inclusion (EII)

In business, as in other aspects of life, we learn and grow from the examples set by others. Imitation can lead to innovation. But how does one decide whom to imitate? And how does one choose which practices to emulate? Imitation cannot occur through mindless conformity. Instead, people must act ethically, creatively, consciously, and responsibly—all while thinking critically. Business ethics refers to implementing appropriate business policies and practices and can be denoted as written or unwritten codes of morals, values, and principles, such as:

- Representative or official responsibility
- Corporate responsibilities
- Organizational loyalties
- Economic responsibilities
- Technical morality
- Legal responsibility

On a personal level, there are also principles that form the basis of business ethics and are what you need to hold yourself accountable to, personal ethics such as:

- Honesty
- Responsibility
- Integrity
- Keeping Your Promises

- Loyalty
- Fairness
- Respect
- Obeying the law

The Leadership Challenge states a mentor is someone who sets clear standards, expects the best, pays attention, personalizes recognition, tells stories and sets examples.[1]

If your mentor doesn't volunteer what is expected of you—ask! Even when learning by example, you need to take responsibility for your own career. Mentors can help you understand your company's values and even formulate your own. If a mentor says, "We focus on client service," ask what that means. If she says, "Our people are our most important asset," determine if those are just words or if they truly reflect reality.

You will look to your mentor as the person who articulates and models the company's values. If your company's ethical standards are going to be meaningful, your mentor should demonstrate those. Your commitment will be greater if you believe the company's values are aligned with your own. The mentoring relationship offers both you and your mentor an opportunity to achieve at a higher level. See Mary Gentile's Giving Voice to Value series, which gives practical ideas and tools to help students (and can apply to mentees, as well) voice their values in real situations.[2]

You should expect your mentor to be a role model. We mirror behavior, not instructions. If your mentor focuses on client service, you will actively replicate the positive way she treats her clients, anticipates their needs, and provides even better service than the client anticipated. If your mentor performs to superior standards, you will likely produce high-quality work. If your mentor doesn't return client phone calls or doesn't give clients regular status updates, you may give client service equally low priority. You want to look up to a mentor who does as she says.

You put a lot of faith in your mentor when you model yourself after her, but trust won't work if it's one-sided. If you don't feel that your mentor trusts you, find out why. You may need to make some changes in order to create that trust. If your mentor needs to be more trusting, tell her that a higher level of trust will propel you toward your goals and a lack of trust impedes your growth. You can even say, "I believe I could be a more confident, valuable employee if you displayed greater confidence in me."

The more praise you get, the better you will perform. Your mentor should know this, but, if she doesn't, remind her! Praise is a powerful tool. Your mentor should not be stingy with it. If you've done a great job, you should be told. Same goes if not. You will accept constructive criticism far easier if appropriate praise is in plentiful supply. Your mentor should be your ally in the company. A combination of elevated expectations—yours and hers—will yield powerful results.

The best mentors pay attention to details and subtleties. If you have built a good relationship, your mentor should be able to determine when trouble is on the horizon. Your mentor should initiate a discussion with the appropriate parties when necessary. It shouldn't be your responsibility alone.

The best mentors can vividly pass along lessons learned. Storytelling has been the principle means by which we have taught one another from the beginning of time so ask your mentor to share her stories. If she needs a bit of nudging, tell her that you will learn more by illustration than instruction. Let her know that you learn more from experience than advice and can reach your own conclusion.

If you have the opportunity to choose your mentor, choose wisely. Great mentors share common traits. There are many, but here are a few I sought in an ethical mentor:

- Is ethical, of course
- Is decisive
- Is trustworthy
- Is even-tempered
- Is genuinely interested
- Is confident
- Is patient
- Gives feedback
- Communicates effectively
- Expresses gratitude
- Shows respect
- Shares knowledge, insights, and ideas
- Responds
- Motivates
- Gives credit

Besides looking for an excellent mentor, you need to be an excellent mentee in order to make the most of your mentoring relationship. Good mentees share several traits:

- You are coachable
- You take responsibility for your career
- You are responsive
- You get to know the mentor as a person
- You give their mentor feedback
- You genuinely want to improve

Who do you know who is successful at what you want to do as you grow in your career? Seek these people out. Determine if they're willing to mentor you. These are the people who will lead with ethics, by example.

Q71 What are the ethics of a responsible mentorship?

By Jason Mollica, Program Director, Online Master's Degree Program in Strategic Communications, American University

Academy Award-winning director Steven Spielberg once said that the delicate balance of mentoring someone is not creating them in your own image but giving them the opportunity to create themselves.[3] This is an important statement because, often, the feeling in mentoring students and professionals is that it is necessary to share our visions on what is right and what is wrong. There's a growing problem, however, when leaders don't uphold the ethical values we have learned.

Sadly, the examples of unethical behavior and practices are all too common. In Major League Baseball, the Houston Astros were punished for creating a sign stealing practice during their World Series run in 2017.[4] Team owner Jim Crane said in a February 2020 press conference that sign stealing didn't impact the game. Nearly a minute later, Crane answered a reporter's question that he never said it didn't impact those games.[5]

There are also the examples of President Donald Trump's actions and statements, on social and digital media, and to the press. President Trump has labeled media outlets as "the enemy" and "fake news"[6] and has taken credit for events that were not of his doing.[7] Imagine being in a classroom and trying to teach the future of the communication industry about ethics when there are perceived leaders acting in an opposite manner. I ask students in my classes, "What can you do if those around you aren't acting ethically?" The given answer is usually to stand up to unethical behavior. But it is not easy to rise and be strong, whether you have experience, or not.

Ethical leadership is defined as "the demonstration of normatively appropriate conduct through personal actions and interpersonal relationships, and the promotion of such conduct to followers through two-way communication, reinforcement, and decision-making."[8] Mentoring students and young professionals is a privilege. I'm passionate about upholding ethical principles. Maybe it was because of what my parents taught me, or what I learned from my grandmother, a legal secretary. She told me that without ethics, we cannot succeed in life or in our careers.

As I entered the consulting world years ago, it was important to create a foundation for ethical behavior. It's called the Four Pillars of Ethics. They are: **Trust, Honesty, Transparency, and Responsibility.** Each pillar supports the others. Without one, your ethical foundation is weakened. Take away two and you can count on a collapse and questions about who you, your brand/organization/company really are to the public.

If we break down each pillar, you can better understand why it takes time to build a strong foundation.

Trust

A very powerful word, which is built through consistency and accuracy. Trust takes years to establish, but mere seconds to destroy. Gaining and keeping trust should be a simple practice. Now, more than ever though, trust is questioned. The Edelman Trust Barometer[9] shows that less than half of the world's mass population trust their institutions to do what is right. When we mentor today's professionals, we take on a great responsibility. Trust leads to open communication. In turn, open communication happens when there is a feeling of safety. As a mentor, take time to listen closely and openly.

Honesty

Billy Joel sang about honesty, saying it's such a lonely word and everyone is untrue. He sang, "Honesty is hardly ever heard and mostly what I need from you." We should always want honesty, even if it is humbling. Sometimes honesty can mean being critical. You should want a frank assessment of your skills, your work, and your direction. You need to be honest with the expectations you have for a project or campaign; the same can be said for mentoring. Our best intention as mentors is to give honest feedback. It may sound harsh. But keep this in mind: we may be the greatest critic, but we are also your biggest fan.

Transparency

It's important that we are clear about the responsibilities we have as mentors. Where do you stand and what do you stand for today? If this isn't clear, you'll lose the attention of a mentee and, possibly, lose out on a chance to make a positive impact. You should never have someone say, "I don't know who they really are and what they represent." We all know someone that says one thing and then does something completely different. That's why transparency is paramount. You need to be clear and concise by not muddying the mentoring waters. Be a two-way communicator. This leads to a culture of openness.

Responsibility

Think for a moment about a time you were counted on to take the lead on a campaign. Maybe you needed to make sure all the social media copy aligned with the overall messaging. *You are the leader*; you are the one the team is looking up to for guidance. As a mentor, you cannot cut corners. You are responsible for who you are and what you do. There is a famous line from Spider-Man, when Uncle Ben tells Peter Parker, "With great power comes great responsibility." If you are given the power of being a mentor, you have people that are depending on you. Never take responsibility for granted. The minute that you take a mentee, or a relationship, for granted, is the moment when that individual realizes you aren't serious about the other three pillars. **Always do the right thing, especially when no one is looking.**

Being ethical should not be understated, just as the importance of mentorship should not. While mentees/mentors may not see the fruits of the relationship right away, the positive impact you work hard to make daily, does set the stage for a more ethical working environment and world.

Q72 Is there a recent question a mentee has asked you about ethics and a challenging communications situation?

By Shonal Burke, President and CEO, Shonali Burke Consulting, Inc.

> "What do you do when you feel the recommendation a senior staffer is providing to your client is not the optimal solution for their needs? But, to speak up would draw their ire and jeopardize your position within your company, potentially to the point of getting sanctioned or, worse yet, fired."

If you have any experience in the agency world, you might just have had a flash of déjà vu. As of this writing (Summer 2020), there could be up to five generations in a workplace.[10] Friction is inevitable, and Millennials, in particular, are frequently on the receiving end of insecurity and fear from their generationally senior counterparts, especially when it comes to their digital prowess. Of course, navigating the corporate jungle is tricky at the best of times; but as technology advances at a breathtaking speed, Millennial employees are frequently faced with the unenviable choice of either heeding their moral compass, or keeping the peace internally.

Such was the dilemma a mentee of mine recently faced. A rising star within her organization, she had been given progressively greater responsibility in her department, managing a key national account, leading communication strategy for the client, as well as hiring, and leading, a growing team of support staff. You could say it was the "perfect" growth trajectory for an ambitious, hardworking, deeply ethical and responsible professional, whose star was rising.

But then, one day, there was an organizational shuffle and, as is all too common when this happens, not only did my mentee's reporting structure change significantly, her department head was now an employee with significant tenure in the organization ... but with absolutely no experience in organizational communication. Uh-oh. How would this go?!

My mentee (let's call her Suzanne which, of course, is nowhere near her real name), was a little nervous. Hitherto she'd enjoyed a good relationship with her new department head (let's call *her* Monica, which, again, is nowhere near *her* real name), as Monica had frequently provided relevant subject matter expertise (SME) for the client's external communications ...

which had been, as you will recall, led by Suzanne. But collaborating as an SME is one thing; how would Monica strategize and lead communications, when that was not her strong suit?

Being a team player, Suzanne created what was, essentially, an onboarding program for Monica. She put together informational documents, went over the nitty-gritties of how things worked with the client, wrote numerous process emails which she routed through *her* supervisor (let's call her Elaine, again not her real name, and who had to manage both up *and* down). In short, she did her best to educate Monica on the *business* of communications, and set her up for success with the client. After all, if Monica succeeded, the entire team did, right?

Unfortunately, Monica was threatened by Suzanne's intelligence, aptitude with communication, *and* excellent client relationship almost immediately … and her ego and insecurity started to get in the way of their work. From the get-go, she would suggest alternative approaches to client work, several of which had been tested earlier on, and dropped in favor of more efficient options. She would offer her opinion on digital and social strategy, without any expertise in the arena, and she started to tacitly encourage the team to "fudge" their timesheets, in order to use up client budget.

For a while, Suzanne tried to respectfully point out to Elaine and Monica why a particular approach might not be the best way to go and provide a viable alternative. It became clear quite early on, though, that this was rubbing Monica the wrong way, who started insinuating that Suzanne was not a "team player." And things started to go south even *more* drastically when Monica started openly "brainstorming" in client meetings … with no prior warning to the team.

Things went from bad to worse, and one day Suzanne called me, almost in tears, asking this very question. Monica was hell-bent on providing the client with a recommendation she knew was sub-par; and not only was she *not* relying on Suzanne for strategic advice (which the client *did*), she was specifically directing her to implement this sub-par solution to the client. This was deeply upsetting to Suzanne, as she was convinced this was not the best use of client time or dollars and could significantly negatively impact the client's campaign. And Elaine didn't seem comfortable respectfully challenging Monica.

Let's step away from this workplace drama for a moment and look at the Code of Ethics of the Public Relations Society of America.[11] It describes numerous core values, including:

- **Honesty.** "We adhere to the highest standards of accuracy and truth in advancing the interests of those we represent and in communicating with the public."
- **Loyalty.** "We are faithful to those we represent, while honoring our obligation to serve the public interest."

There are several others, but I think these two are particularly pertinent in this situation.

Now, put yourself in Suzanne's shoes for a minute. She's faced with a situation where she is representing both her employer *and* her client (the "honesty" core value). Further, "loyalty" would certainly indicate that she not subvert her department head in any way, even unintentionally. Not only would that be morally reprehensible, it could also jeopardize the agency-client relationship.

Further, one *could* argue that Monica was doing the best that she possibly could; she just didn't have the expertise to make an optimal recommendation to the client ... but was it really Suzanne's place to call that out? What about Elaine (who reported to Monica)—what was her role here? And why had the agency reorganization resulted in Monica being given leadership of the department, when she clearly lacked the skills, expertise, *and* experience to lead Elaine, Suzanne, and the team in this capacity?

It is precisely this kind of situation that underscores how vital a role the public relations counselor plays in an organization, or with clients. While most of us are not trained to be therapists or lawyers, we inevitably have to use our listening skills, intuition, logic, and judgement to give our employers or clients our best recommendations to communicate efficiently *and* ethically. Most importantly, we have to be able to live with our recommendations ... which means the most important person we answer to is ourselves.

What advice would you give Suzanne?

Would you advise her to throw Monica under the bus, as it were, and contradict her recommendations to the client?

Or would you advise her to argue with Elaine and Monica as to the best course of action, out of client earshot (ideally), at the risk of being sanctioned internally ... or even losing her job?

Or would you advise her to do nothing? Or something else entirely?

The fact is that reality is never easy to deal with, and in a situation like this, there is no real "win-win." With Suzanne already enduring covert harassment at work, her already stressful work life would have become even more miserable had she dug her heels in with Monica.

And directly contradicting Monica in front of Elaine and/or the client could certainly be construed as disloyal, not to mention rude and disrespectful.

Ultimately, Suzanne raised her concerns with Elaine (with whom she did have a good relationship), and then relinquished ownership of the outcome. She had followed both her conscience, as well as the appropriate "chain of command." In other words, she did everything it was appropriate for her to do. She behaved honestly, loyally, *and* ethically; she had done the best she could do, and was *appropriate* for her to do, given the extremely challenging situation.

And the next day she started looking for a new job.

Q73 What is the best piece of ethics advice from a mentor?

By Martin Waxman, President, Martin Waxman Communications

As someone who's had a 26+ year career in public relations—and always considered myself an ethical communicator—I haven't known my ethics mentor for that long, and yet his influence on me has been wide-ranging.

We actually met a few years ago when I went back to school to complete my Master of Communications Management degree from McMaster and Syracuse universities. One of the courses in the curriculum focused on theoretical and applied business ethics. I teach reputation management and felt I would have something useful to contribute to this class. I've also advised both clients and students to default to an honest and ethical approach when confronted by a significant issue. And of course, that is important.

But I soon learned I was lacking a key component of ethical decision-making. While I considered myself objective, I based difficult decisions on my own past experience and gut. I didn't have anything resembling a strategic approach to draw on.

But I'm getting a bit ahead of myself.

At this point, let me introduce my mentor, one of the smartest and most empathetic communications strategists and professors I know. Many of you may already have met or heard of him, and if you have, I think you'll agree with my assessment.

His name is Michael Meath.

Michael has had a successful career in business and communications that spanned over 30 years, during which time he counseled CEOs, started and ran his own agency, and was both a communications professor and the head of the public relations and communications program at Syracuse University S.I. Newhouse School of Communication.

Michael taught us why we need to adopt a formalized ethical decision-making roadmap and not simply rely on our values and what we believe may be right. The starting point, he said, was understanding what ethics is—a system that helps us differentiate between right and wrong, fair and unfair, good and bad. Michael provided a framework we could use to put an ethical decision-making process into practice.

And it all began with four simple words: **Hit the Pause Button.**

I know. It almost seems too easy. But let's "pause" a moment to consider what it means.

In any issue or crisis situation, our normal impulse is to jump into the deep end without considering what the water may be like when we land. And that could mean we're unprepared for many unpredictable variables like the freezing temperature we didn't expect or that there's a dangerous undercurrent swirling underneath.

But stopping—even for a few critical moments—and taking a step back step back to reflect on the situation and its possible causes and repercussions, could help you gain a clearer and calmer head. It also gives you an opportunity to develop a more objective view of the situation you or your organization might be facing.

In essence, you're slowing things down, even though that may feel counterintuitive to do in the middle of a crisis that could be unfolding at breakneck speed.

By following Michael's advice, you're giving yourself and your team an opportunity to shift from the anxiety of the moment to a place where you can begin to formulate a more strategic response, one designed to rebuild relationships, repair reputation damage, and restore the business to its "normal" state of affairs.

Hitting the pause button gives perspective, at a 50,000-foot view, of the pressure points that may be affecting your organization, both from the outside and inside. You can then examine a myriad of strategic considerations and develop and play out scenarios and the possible short and long-term consequences for each. And you can review the obligations you may with your stakeholders that could help you determine what the optimal next steps might be. This happens quickly and becomes the foundation of the process.

You will also need to learn about and select whether you will be taking a deontological or duty-based approach grounded in morality, a teleological or utilitarian approach that weighs the consequences and chooses the road that causes the most good for the most people, or possibly a hybrid of the two.

And if you haven't had the opportunity to do so, I urge you to take some time and delve into ethics in communications and learn how to adopt an ethical decision-making process that's not solely reliant on your intuition and beliefs. Instead, adopt a strategy that, as Michael Meath says, will "reduce emotional pressure" so you and your team can "make the 'best right decision'" for the circumstances you are facing.

Q74 What can you share about your experience with ethical mentoring?

By Anthony D'Angelo, APR, Fellow PRSA, Professor of Practice,
S.I. Newhouse School of Public Communications, Syracuse University

Serving as a mentor in an ethically responsible way, or as a mentor engaging on the subject of ethics with a mentee, are responsibilities I take to heart. In fact, failing to uphold them would break my heart because they are so important to the connections I strive to have with people, and to their careers and personal lives.

Ethical mentoring is indeed serious stuff. Seriously influential, necessary, valuable, educational and rewarding for both parties; often challenging and strenuous; sometimes frustrating and disappointing—it is like most activities of great worth. One also improves with study and practice, and fortunately there are excellent reference sources available and even more numerous opportunities to exercise mentoring disciplines for almost anyone in any organization.

Mentorship is a learning venture for both parties, and while no one learns it all, the opportunity to continuously improve is deeply rewarding. As someone who is a work in progress, I would offer the following principles that I've learned and shared.

The first is a condition of many games of chance that I heard from a mentor of mine, public relations counselor and former PRSA National Chair Gary McCormick: you have to be present to win. Being present is also essential to ethical and effective mentoring because without being fully present you can't be fully engaged, and if you're not fully engaged, you're cheating the other party, whether mentee or mentor. By engagement, I mean you should care about the other, what they're striving for, what they hope to gain. You must listen actively, for what they're saying and why they're saying it. You must work hard to earn empathy, even with a mentee who is quite different from you, because, once earned, empathy is the key to deeper understanding and influence.

To enter a mentoring relationship with pre-formed or surface-level answers or advice is to devalue that relationship. Despite your professional experience and potential ability to give experienced advice, mentoring is not just about you or your protégé, it's about committing to a relationship.

Mentoring is indeed a relationship, not a transaction. I can write a career advice column and post it somewhere, and that can be valuable but it's not mentoring. It may help people, but it's not personal, and mentoring is personal. A relationship is mutual and has duration. There is bilateral give and take. Another mentor of mine, the legendary Pat Jackson, founder of Jackson, Jackson & Wagner, used to say, "People want to be involved, not told; served not sold." It's one of the most valuable phrases I've ever learned.

It means that people are influenced by others involving them, not ordering or directing. And they intuitively know if you are sincerely addressing their needs or merely trying to sell them something. Jackson held that if you involve someone in addressing a situation of mutual interest you can co-author a solution together. This generates powerful buy-in, and often, a better solution as the result of generous collaboration. Getting involved with people is labor-intensive and demands patience. The rewards, however, can be enormously gratifying and enrich both mentor and mentee.

We must know those ethical principles we will employ and defend, every day, forever. The public relations profession cannot afford fluidity of ethical standards, lest practitioners become like the Groucho Marx joke, "Those are my principles, and if you don't like them ... well, I have others."

Ethically challenging situations can vary greatly and have myriad complicating factors, which is why subscribing to a defined code of ethics is critical. The Public Relations Society of America's Code of Ethics, The Arthur W. Page Society's Page Principles and the Global Alliance's Global Principles of Ethics provide thoroughly researched and carefully considered frameworks for professional ethics. Communications professionals should commit to one of these codes, know it thoroughly and practice it diligently with the knowledge that comes from examining case studies.

Mentoring works best when both parties enter into it with humility and openness to mutual change. It is not false modesty for even an experienced mentor to recognize that she or he does not have all or even most of the answers and may be insufficiently equipped to guide a mentee who is facing a challenge or dilemma. That's actually a strength and can be the foundation for a relationship where mentor and protégé explore situations together, compare impressions and discuss concerns. If I'm the mentor I may have some experience of value, but I've found that mentoring is more about helping people discover the best direction for themselves rather than simply saying "do this."

It's been my experience that mentees already know most if not all of the aspects required to come to an ethical decision, and that I could be most helpful by assisting them in organizing and applying their own thoughts and feelings.

I do think mentees have a right to expect confidentiality in the relationship, because trust is essential to it. For that reason, I believe anyone approaching me seeking ethical guidance can be completely candid about any suspicions or misgivings concerning ethical conditions in their organization, or mine. If someone says they suspect wrongdoing but don't know what to do about it or have evidence of unethical behavior but are concerned about repercussions from reporting it, I would want to ensure they have a safe opportunity to assess the situation thoroughly and perhaps more objectively than they could on their own.

I don't believe it's necessarily required for a mentor to have industry- or business-specific knowledge in order to guide a person through an ethical dilemma. As a communications industry veteran I'm most knowledgeable and experienced in ethical communications principles and codes but have found that they are often applicable across an array of industries and businesses. While there may be technical or industry-specific considerations that are factors in a particular business's ethical challenge, our profession's ethical codes are industry-agnostic. If I were not knowledgeable about an industry or business, it would be an opportunity for me to learn from the mentee about the specific situation and hopefully engage in a more robust dialogue involving ethical principles as they would apply in that case. That's not to say I assume I can assist anyone in any industry with any ethical dilemma. If I felt ill-equipped or had misgivings about being able to help, I would tell the mentee so and turn my attention to finding someone who might be better suited.

Q75 What are the kinds of questions you can ask a mentor (in confidence) about ethics or an ethical challenge you are facing?

By Gini Dietrich, founder of Spin Sucks and CEO, Arment Dietrich

Early in my career, a client asked me if I could call a politician's office and pose as a reporter to ask some questions and try to get some traction for an issue they were working on. I knew it was unethical and I did not feel comfortable doing that, but I also was early enough in my career to not have the confidence or courage to tell the client no. Thankfully I had a mentor who helped me navigate the issue with my boss—and then with the client. My boss and I together presented some options without straight out telling him no.

This is the kind of relationship that is a must for everyone in their career. As you're starting out, it's to help you craft the right kind of delivery, so everyone wins. As your career grows, it's to have someone to gut check your instinct.

Oftentimes the conversations you'll have with your mentor are around a specific incident, but if you have a true mentor relationship, you'll be meeting monthly (or more) and won't always have a specific incident to discuss.

In those cases, it's always interesting to dissect current events. You could talk about what's happening in the world and whether or not you agree with how it's being handled. Also read the PR blogs that speak to ethics for fodder.

Some good places to start are with the types of questions you might be asked during an interview:

- Tell me about a time you were faced with an ethical dilemma and how you handled it.
- What's your idea of an ethical organization?
- Have you ever suffered in your career for doing what was right?
- If your boss asked you to lie for them, what would you do?
- How does value relate to ethics?
- What is meant by ethics?
- Should there be ethics in technology?
- What is the point of ethics?

From there, you can get into more philosophical questions, such as:

- What harsh truths do you prefer to ignore?
- Is free will real or just an illusion?
- Is there a meaning to life? If so, what is it?
- Where is the line between art and not art?
- What should be the goal of humanity?
- Does fate exist? If so, do we have free will?
- What does it mean to live a good life?
- Why do we dream?
- Where does your self-worth come from?
- How will humans as a species become extinct?

Those questions aren't related to business, necessarily, but they will help you figure out where your own values lie, what's important to you in your career, and what you won't stand for.

And then you can move into the current events with questions such as:

- Is there harm in "fake news"? Why or why not?
- How do you think the country should handle a White House press secretary who is caught in a lie?
- Is it permissible to torture one person to obtain the happiness of many?
- Why should I respect the intellectual rights of others?
- Do I have a duty to help others?
- Do I have a duty to assist the police?
- Do I have a moral obligation to boycott that business?
- How do I stand up for what I believe in?
- Can I join that movement without losing my job?

There are ethical dilemmas all around us, every day. Throughout your career you'll be tested with minor things—and by major things. Having a mentor to help you work through things and find solutions—and sometimes even helping to figure out a way to communicate something uncomfortable—is one of the best investments you can make in your career.

Q76 Can you ask your mentor to help you clean up an unethical situation and to help spread accurate information for you?

By Ken Jacobs, CEO, Jacobs Consulting & Executive Coaching

That's a thought-provoking question. Actually, two thought-provoking questions, which encourage even further questions.

First, as to "cleaning up" an unethical situation, it's important to clarify if you made the potentially unethical situation, or if you believe your organization did.

If you made the misstep, it's not the mentor's responsibility to clean it up, nor to spread accurate information for you. It is your responsibility to own up to what you did, make a sincere apology, and clarify what proper ethical behavior you'll implement going forward. You can, and probably should get your mentor's counsel on how to do this so that you can effectively move on, with lessons learned.

In addition, it may be a good time to review how you behave on a regular basis, and if your actions are in lockstep with your ethical "North Star." Think back to the penultimate scene in the movie "The Devil Wears Prada," when the villain of the piece, Miranda Priestly, played by Meryl Streep, is riding in a limousine with the protagonist, Andy, played by Anne Hathaway. Miranda tells Andy, she sees a lot of herself in her, in reference to Andy making the choice *not* to say "No" when Miranda told her to do something that was clearly ethically wrong. At that point, Andy gets out of the limousine, and throws her mobile phone away in anger.

Does Andy do this because she disagrees with Miranda's assessment? I don't think so. I say it's because she knows Miranda is right, that for the sake of her career Andy has walked away from her guiding principles.

In sum, make sure that you're walking in lockstep with yours.

If you believe the organization acted in an unethical manner, it would be prudent to ask yourself a number of questions.

1) Did the organization truly act in an unethical manner, or is that my interpretation of it? What are other possible interpretations?

Let me be clear, this isn't about excusing unethical behavior. Not at all. Just making sure that if we're going to take some action, we've looked at it in multiple ways. Our perceptions become our reality, so they're critically important. In addition, we often see what we look for. As such, it's imperative to look at this from a multitude of views before determining the appropriate action.

2) Did the organization do something in violation of its ethical values? Or your own?

Sometimes we hold our organizations, our family, and friends to our ethical principles. But does it make sense to do that? Let's not hold others responsible for abiding by contracts they haven't signed.

If that's the case, it's time to examine the space between your values and your company's values are, and to do a little introspective thinking. We do best in our careers when the majority of our organization's values align with our own. It doesn't have to be all of them, but it does have to be a clear majority of them, and especially around the big values. While some start with an organization where there is a gap between their values and the organization's, usually for economic reasons, be warned that this isn't sustainable. Sooner rather than later, you'll likely have an "Andy" moment.

But it's not just about avoiding that moment: When we work for companies with whom there is values alignment, we're more engaged, we're inspired, we're more motivated and passionate about our work.

In my experience, that helps us lead a life of enjoyment, fulfillment, success, and abundance, and yes, economic abundance. It often takes a little research to find an organization with whom we share a majority of important values, and courage to leave one where our values aren't in sync.

And it's well worth doing.

3) What are my organization's policies in respect to how it handles potentially unethical behavior, either by an individual or the organization itself? What is the process HR uses to investigate these kinds of allegations?

Part of that equation is knowing if confidentiality is guaranteed, and what sorts of protections are offered to whistleblowers. This is something you should be able to easily determine. I would do my best to understand these in full before proceeding.

And I believe this is an area worth discussing with one's mentor. Should you decide to do so, I'd recommend bringing this up in terms of believing or suspecting someone might have acted in an unethical way. Don't be judge and jury all in one. It's acceptable to provide benefit of the doubt, until an investigation proves unethical behavior.

As to the question of should you ask your mentor to help spread accurate information for you, as someone who's mentored many PR and communications professionals, both formally and informally, I'm not sure that that's their role.

According to PRSANY, for which I served on the Mentoring Committee and have served as a mentor for many years, mentors share their wisdom with the next generation, give lessons that will last over the lifetimes of their careers, and provide individualized attention and objective counsel, among other things.

But there's no mention there, or anywhere else that I could find for that matter, of having to spread accurate information about their "mentee."

That said, one of the things a mentor can do is discuss the following with their mentee:

- The importance of having multiple supporters in an organization, beyond one's supervisor/leader.
- How to build one's influence throughout an organization.
- How one can lead up, across, and down.

- And how one can build, protect, and defend one's reputation as an ethical practitioner of communications, and in all things.

Those, to me, align much better with a classic definition of a mentor than the notion of spreading information, accurate though it may be, and is ultimately more beneficial to the mentee.

In reviewing all my answers above, a number of things I've always believed about how to make ethical decisions stand out:

- Making ethical decisions isn't always easy.
- Question, question, and questions some more.
- Always make sure you are following your own personal ethics North Star.
- Don't make assumptions about others' ethical behavior, including the organization where you work. Be willing to look at all things from multiple angles before making your decision.
- It's okay if all this makes one uncomfortable.

The Marketing Experts "Weigh In" on Ethical Guidance

Training the Ethical Mind

By Mark McClennan, APR, Fellow PRSA, General Manager of C+C's Boston Office

People are five times more likely to make an ethical decision when they are given time to think, according to a seminal study from the Academy of Management.[12] Yet when it comes to marketing and communications, we are rarely given as much time as we need to think, plan, respond and act, so we make snap judgements. It is when we make these snap judgements that people tend to make the most common ethical missteps.

The solution to this is to train our ethical mind. By regularly discussing ethical scenarios and issues with a mentor, professionals can better prepare themselves to make ethical decisions under pressure.

Mentors are an essential element in the development of ethical reasoning and are a sounding board for difficult situations. I have spoken with hundreds of executives for Ethical Voices, and they all invariably have a piece of ethical advice they received from a mentor that helped shape their ethics outlook and approach to business. Some of the advice was profound, some very practical, but all of it came from a senior executive (or a parent) and shaped their character for decades to come.

Mentors also serve as a go to resource when executives find themselves with difficult decisions to make. While often a spouse or partner serves in that role, mentors bring greater relevant expertise with almost the same level of trust and confidence.

Mentors are typically a trusted, senior practitioner. Having a boss as a mentor can be effective, but there is always the underlying tension of the manager/employee relationship. So, for many people, mentors are best found outside their chain of command. Or at least people look to a second mentor with whom they an confide if there are issues too sensitive to bring to their manager. At agencies that can be relatively simple to do, but in corporate or non-profit jobs where the teams may be smaller, it may be more challenging. This is where associations like PRSA, the AMA and the PRSA College of Fellows can help. Local or section meetings can be a great place to make connections and find a mentor.

When it comes to finding an ethics mentor, it is essential to truly understand the underlying approach the mentor takes to evaluating an ethical decision and make sure it matches your own. If your mentor takes a duty-based approach (and act is either ethical or unethical based on the nature of the act), and you follow a utilitarian model (the greatest good for the greatest number), you may well have different takes on the situation. No ethical model is perfect, they all have their drawbacks. But understanding how you and your mentor approach a situation is essential for evaluating their advice.

One key point to being an effective ethics mentor. The strongest lessons are those that the mentees learn themselves. I teach ethics at Boston University and have managed agency teams for decades. I quickly learned that giving an ethics problem and solution is the least effective way to teach and mentor. It is more effective to raise the issue and drive discussion. Help people work through the implications of their decisions. Help them understand why good people may come to different ethical decisions and how you work with that. That is why invariably when someone asks me a question, my first response is almost always "what do you think?" It helps crystallize the situation and sets the framework for the discussion.

Keep in mind though, there is no attorney/client or even agency/client relationship between you and your mentor. You need to be careful what confidential details you share with them. When dealing with a sensitive issue it is best not to use real names or specific IP.

In the end, mentors are coaches, but it is the individual practitioner that will need to make the call. Seek advice, you are not alone. But when it comes time to make the call, the only one that can do that is you – through your action or inaction.

Mentorship for Rising Professionals

By Karen Freberg, Author and Associate Professor of Strategic Communication, University of Louisville

Mentorship is one of the most important, yet overlooked, areas we are seeing in the industry across the board. A mentor is someone who not only has the experience and expertise in the field, but they have the commitment and generosity in taking time out to help give back to the profession and pay it forward. In my role as a professor, I take mentorship and the role it plays in my profession very seriously.

There are many characteristics on what makes a great mentor, which for rising professionals entering the field. First, the willingness to share expertise, experiences (good and bad) and expertise with others. We all learn from examples and stories other share—and a strong mentor is someone who is willing to share these openly with key lessons learned along the way. Second, a mentor also knows when they can be mentored as well. Reverse mentorship is a beautiful thing, and we can all learn from each other. A mentor could find themselves in a situation where they are asking the person they are mentoring for help. Even as a professor, I constantly learn so much from my students as they bring forth new perspectives, trends, and insights into the classroom.

A successful mentor is open to learning from all sides of the coin, because this is all part of the growing and evolving process. They take a personal interest in being a positive role model. Actions speak louder than words, and sometimes we forget what we do is what others see, rather than what we say. This is a key point here for marketers to note. Someone could say the best and most wonderful things about what they can do to help you, but at the end of the day, if they are not willing to take actions, they are missing the boat on a great opportunity to help someone. Mentors value learning and growth from different sources and encourages lifelong learning. In our industry, if we are not dedicated in our studies on the current issues, challenges, and trends in the field, we may as well retire and call it a day. Learning is crucial for success, and a mentor is not only encouraging this for their mentees, but they are also doing it themselves to show they are not just passing along advice, but they are living it as well.

Providing constructive yet impactful feedback is one way a mentor can help. Bouncing around ideas about work, practice, or certain situations and how to handle them is one of the ways a mentor can provide guidance and advice. Sometimes, this advice is real and straight to the point, which may come across to some as harsh. The goal of a mentor is not to sugar coat things—but to provide insights and perspective that may be valuable and not disillusion the mentee with a false pretense. In my classes, I tell my students my goal is not to present a picture-perfect situation all the time for the industry or to describe the perfect organization or agency to work in. It's important to give them insights and experiences they need to know and be aware of, so they are not caught off guard.

Some questions you can ask your mentor on ethical situations include:

- What are the ramifications of reporting this ethical issue internally?

- How will this ethical situation impact my career?
- What steps should I take to address this situation?

One important element to note here is to remember that a mentor's reward is seeing you succeed. My Dad had a saying in track and field when he was my coach that when I was on the award stand getting my first-place medal in track and field, he joked how there wasn't an award stand for coaches or medals they won. The reward was seeing me succeed and achieve my goals. A true mentor wants you to succeed—knowing that they are not the ones in the spotlight. The true reward is knowing you have made an impact on someone's life for the better.

Being a mentor is one of the biggest honors anyone can have. The ability to make an impact and difference in someone's life is truly amazing. One of the best things about my work as a professor is helping others. Mentorship is a crucial part of modern marketing practices and finding the person to help you in this journey is an exciting and rewarding experience.

Notes

1 J. M. Kouzes & B. Z. Posner, *The Leadership Challenge*. John Wiley & Sons, August 2007.
2 Mary Gentile, "Giving Voice to Values," Darden School of Business, University of Virginia, https://www.darden.virginia.edu/ibis/initiatives/gvv, August 2020.
3 Colin D. Ellis, *The Project Book: The Complete Guide to Consistently Delivering Great Projects*. John Wiley & Sons, June 2019.
4 Neil Vigdor, "The Houston Astros' Cheating Scandal: Sign-Stealing, Buzzer Intrigue and Tainted Pennants," New York Times, https://www.nytimes.com/article/astros-cheating.html, February 2020.
5 Scott Davis, "The Astros say their cheating scandal 'didn't impact the game' and players shouldn't be held accountable in a cringeworthy press conference," Business Insider, https://www.businessinsider.com/jim-crane-astros-cheating-didnt-impact-game-press-conference-2020-2, February 2020.
6 Jacqueline Howard & Daniel Dale, "Trump takes credit for decline in cancer deaths. The American Cancer Society says he's wrong," CNN, https://www.cnn.com/2020/01/09/politics/cancer-deaths-trump-fact-check-bn/index.html, January 2020.
7 Manuel Roig-Franzia & Sarah Ellison, "A history of the Trump War on Media—the obsession not even coronavirus could stop," Washington Post, https://www.washingtonpost.com/lifestyle/media/a-history-of-the-trump-war-on-media—the-obsession-not-even-coronavirus-could-stop/2020/03/28/71bb21d0-f433-11e9-8cf0-4cc99f74d127_story.html, March 2020.
8 M. E. Brown, L. K. Treviño, & D. A. Harrison, "Ethical leadership: a social learning perspective for construct development and testing." *Organ. Behav. Hum. Dec. Process.* 97(2), pp. 117–134, June 2005. DOI: 10.1016/j.obhdp.2005.03.002.
9 Edelman Trust Barometer, https://www.edelman.com/trustbarometer, January 2020.

10 Greg Pryor, "Generational Differences and the Shifting Workplace," Forbes, https://www.forbes.com/sites/workday/2019/09/12/generational-differences-and-the-shifting-workplace/#ed0692f53ce7, September 2019.
11 PRSA Code of Ethics, About Section, https://www.prsa.org/about/ethics/prsa-code-of-ethics, August 2020.
12 Brian C. Gunia et al., "Contemplation and Conversation: Subtle Influences on Moral Decision Making," Academy of Management Journal 55, pp. 13–33, February 2012.

Chapter 7

Being a Leader Means Being an Ethical Role Model

In 1925, Napoleon Hill wrote his book, *The Law of Success*. The Fifth Law or lesson, entitled Initiative and Leadership, focuses on all of the qualities of a successful leader. At one point in the lesson, Hill shares what he deems "The Call for New Leaders and a New Brand of Leadership."[1] He presents 20 Leadership Qualities for readers to understand the meaning and responsibility that comes with leading people. The list also evaluates a person's individual qualities against the 20 characteristics presented. These characteristics range from self-confidence, self-control and accurate thinking to the tolerance, temperance and the harmony leaders should possess. Reading the list, it becomes clear how many of the attributes relate to ethics and values, which helps to foster good judgment in decision-making.

If Hill were alive today, would his prediction ring true for a new brand of leaders and leadership? Visionary leaders rise to the top of their organizations ready to face challenges every day. Their path can be winding with pressures, issues, and unexpected situations to test their ethics and values. What kind of leadership qualities do you possess? Understanding your own leadership style, practices, decision-making processes, and the qualities that guide you are what help to shape your actions and outcomes for others.

At the same time, surrounding yourself with professionals who have the best interest of the people they serve also becomes a dominant factor. In social psychology, the term crowd or "mob" psychology can affect your behavior and how you think and perform in your own professional role. Hill also points out how the people who are a part of your business, whether it is your customers or partners in the business, with a greater investment and a cooperative type of crowd psychology, perhaps a new brand of ethical leaders can be nurtured.

Along the same lines, if you are a leader, or you are aspiring to lead in your organization, then you are being watched closely. As you demonstrate your leadership skills, professionals around you, including your peers and subordinates, will take your leadership cues by adopting the vision you set forth and incorporating the values and ethics you display into their own practices. With this responsibility, there is no skimping or cutting of the ethical corners. It goes back to what was stated earlier in the book's Introduction, you are either ethical or you are not. There is no middle of the road or an in between. If you call yourself a leader, then doing what is best for the people around you (all of them) has to come first. You would acknowledge that focusing solely on what your shareholders or Board of Directors want the most, does not necessarily benefit **all** of the groups you serve.

What makes an ethical leader and how do you place your ethics and your good judgment in decision-making above all else? There are plenty of tests that let you know the type of person you are, and which also identify your strengths as a business professional. One of my favorite assessments is the 16 Personality Types test. Myers and Briggs created the evaluation also to point out the differences in the people around you. Of course, there are other tests including the DISC Profile, based on four behaviors including Dominance, Influence, Steadiness, and Compliance. There is also StrengthsFinder, which is the popular assessment used by Gallup. StrengthsFinder uncovers your five core strengths out of a possible 34 strengths you may possess.

However, can self-assessment always be the defining factor as to how you will lead? For example, if you are sharing your assessment for a job interview, or as a part of a professional group, do you give others the "real" you, or the version of who you would like to be? Only you can answer this question. Of course, a test is a test, and self-evaluation is tremendously helpful when YOU want to know who you are.

If ethics and values are a personal choice and you demonstrate ethical conduct outside of work, then can it be argued that you are more likely to take those same beliefs and good conduct into your work life too? If you are living the real you, then ethics and values will show up both in a personal sense and as a business priority too. Here is the real test: Do you make ethics a personal choice and business practice? The most effective leaders, who are not separating their work life and personal life behavior, want everyone to know who they really are!

The questions and answers in this chapter focus on leaders who want to take the lead and be responsible as Ethical Marketers and communication role models. They know ethics and values are a part of their DNA not just some of the time, but all of the time. Of course, not everyone will be happy when you practice your ethics and values, weighing different situations to benefit the most people involved or based on your duty as a leader. However, your integrity will remain intact, and a valuable lesson can always be learned.

The leaders who want their people and their constituents to thrive are the professionals who lead with values of the heart and with ethics on their minds.

Q77 How much does the human and the transparency in communication help leaders to build trust?

You paint a picture of yourself every day, whether you realize it or not. Your verbal and non-verbal communication are being picked up, analyzed and decoded by all of your employees and every constituent group you serve. In order to build trust with the people who surround you, the human and the transparent parts of your commanding presence have to be visible, at all times.

What does it mean to be human and transparent and why is it so hard for some professionals to incorporate these traits into their communication and their roles? Do you remember when social media was just coming into the spotlight? Many company executives were refusing to participate. They also frowned upon their employees or company departments participating in social media communities. I delivered many lectures on why social media participation was good for a business. These leaders were used to and comfortable with "controlling" the narrative, framing specifically what people should say inside of the company, as well as the discussions extending beyond their own organizations online and in different social communities.

In 2000, *The Cluetrain Manifesto*, written by Rick Levine, Christopher Locke, Doc Searls, and David Weinberger, pointed out how business leaders never really had control of what was being shared by their employees. There were still conversations around the "water cooler" and in the hallways of their companies.[2] It was the understanding that information will get out, whether it was quickly or in a "drip drip" fashion. Information, news, and stories, were, without a doubt, going to see the light of day and be shared internally and publicly too.

The leaders who decided to show up to social media with their human side, and who were more vulnerable and transparent with their people, became the clear winners in the trust-building department. When you are **not** willing to share in a human and transparent fashion, especially on social media, you may actually be fueling the negative, the distrust and the communication issues that surface publicly. Withholding information, not informing your people and the public regularly and/or taking steps to shut down communication and not correcting the record when misinformation runs rampant, are the opposite of what people expect from their transparent leaders.

To build up trust and confidence with your employees, leaders must:

- Share the good news often, and also the not-so-good situations that go on within their companies. Sharing with transparency builds trust with your people. When you trust your people with all kinds of information, you will also learn the importance of educating them on how to share appropriately.

- Be willing to have clear, concise, and open dialogue around topics that affect employees and other important stakeholder groups. Sometimes the topics you want to avoid that are trending in the news are also surfacing within your company and need to be addressed with empathy and understanding.
- Learn to use transparency as a way to empower others to be optimistic on subjects that are often dismissed or not brought out in the open. When the conversation flows constructively, and people feel they can share and be heard, you will see an increase in motivation and productivity.
- Communicate frequently to keep people in the loop and feeling connected with the company beyond their own departments. Giving people more information in a timely fashion is always appreciated and is a sign that you believe in them. They, in return, will invest in the company and their leadership team.

Being transparent and human means being more comfortable, open and willing to share what are more challenging subjects. Remember, the days of "controlling," even before social media, never worked for an organization and its leaders—the truth eventually comes out.

If what is being shared by leaders does not meet the expectations of their people, because the human and the transparent are missing, then chances are the trust does not grow or will eventually break down over time.

Q78 Should leaders share situations that are ethically challenging or times when good judgment has not been exercised?

I remember reading Hélio (Fred) Garcia's book, *The Agony of Decision*. In the book, Fred discusses the Golden Hour of Crisis Response[3]. Granted, not every challenging ethical issue turns into a situation of crisis proportions. However, there is an important lesson in Garcia's teachings. He shares in his book, four critical questions to ask in that first hour. The first question really speaks to the extent of sharing the challenging situations for a company. The question is: Will those who matter to us expect us to do or say something now?

What a thought-provoking question and one that clearly comes from a place of what is best for the people and not necessarily the leaders running the company, or its Board of Directors and the shareholders. Garcia also shares in his book and on social media that leaders need to base their responses on what reasonable people would expect from a reasonable company. The answer to this question is also your guide or compass as to when you should share. Of course, you are also keeping in mind there are certain timing issues when organizations and professionals are prohibited from sharing, which protects the public they serve from additional damage or future harm.

Now, you can think about challenging situations and your leaders. How have they handled past communications, ethically or unethically? Was the communications decision based on the people who matter and what did those reasonable people expect? Being in one too many crisis meetings, I have always operated under the "tell your story first" principle, to be truthful and transparent, and to get ahead of someone else sharing in a much less flattering way.

Transparency and accepting accountability are two criteria which are imperative for today's leaders. These two characteristics are not reserved for the good times only. Remember them, and better yet, practice them when situations are more challenging, and when decisions are pressing and will impact your people and the public.

Q79 When you're a leader, what does it mean to be an ethical role model?

Being an ethical role model does not mean you have to be perfect. As a matter of fact, I don't know many leaders who are perfect in their personal, professional and mentoring roles. The notion of "perfect" really does not exist. Leaders are human and they, too, are allowed to make mistakes. The goal is to learn from every single misstep and to be honest with your mentees, employees, or the people who look up to you; the goal is to score high on the truth and accountability scale.

However, there are certain qualities you would hope a leader has and your ethical role models possess. For me, it has always been a blend of Intelligence Quotient (IQ) and Emotional Quotient (EQ) qualities along with a good dose of accountability. On the IQ side, I have admired role models and leaders who were innovative, intelligent, critical thinkers, confident and visionary. On the EQ side, I have been drawn to leaders and role models who are not frightened to show their human and genuine side. They build relationships through their ability to be transparent and open with the people who look up to them. These leaders are also emotionally intelligent with a good handle on their own emotions, so they are able to manage the emotions of others. They display self-control and a lot of self-awareness in all of their interactions.

Being an ethical role model is also an opportunity to take the best qualities of your own mentors and draw what you can from different leaders around you. It is the old saying, "always know your audience." You will consult with certain people when you want to tap into their strengths. I have also recognized that not every mentor and role model is well suited for each problem you encounter in business.

Just know that an ethical role model will step up to the plate and bring the best intentions and advice forward. Take their expertise and advice with gratitude, focusing on what you need. You can learn from the stories and insights different leaders and mentors share, based on their personal and professional experiences.

Q80 Are the ethical standards for the leaders at a higher level?

There may be varying opinions about the answer to the question. However, why should someone lead if he or she is not held to the highest standard? With leadership come big expectations and the responsibility to the people in their organizations and all of the groups they serve. Why would we call someone a leader if they did not uphold the highest ethical standards? After all, if leaders were not held to higher standards then their position would appear to be more about power and authority, and less about integrity and character and in best interest of the people who rely on the organization.

As mentioned, the word "leadership" implies expectations. When you think of leaders, who do you want to follow, believe in and/or entrust your safety and well-being? What qualities are you looking for in this professional? I am looking for honesty and integrity. I also want to know leaders are respectful and patient. They should inspire and empower others as they demonstrate their own level of commitment and passion. If every leader were to act like a mentor, investing personally in each person that relies on them for information, then we would see a difference in our leaders and the way they operate companies in the market today.

So yes, leaders should be held to higher standards and here is where their standards exceed others:

- Leaders lead from within; they have a guiding compass to help, and to do no harm.
- Leaders make a commitment and stick with it; they are not looking for the exit or to give up when challenges surface.
- Leaders live by a code with you and for you; there is one set of standards and they know they are accountable for meeting these standards too.
- Leaders always take the high road; honesty, integrity and respect are high on their list of character traits.
- Leaders serve with a strong presence and a loving heart; they are not afraid to show their confidence and intelligence, yet their sensitivities come through as they can be vulnerable too.

What separates leaders from everyone else is their ability to go above and beyond and to *show* others their best practices, not just talk about them. Actions speak louder than words, whether it is in policy, procedures, or everyday interactions.

Leaders are the compass of an organization, and they need to direct, guide and be the beacon of hope for the rest of the employees who will follow their lead. Promoting good conduct starts from the top down and inside out. Otherwise, you may encounter that familiar and unpleasant expression, "The fish rots from the head."

Q81 Is there ever a time that leaders should step down in protest of an ethical challenge?

If you are a leader, then you have a choice, and stepping down in protest is absolutely one of those choices. There are several examples of leaders putting their conscience and values first, before propagating or carry out policies and initiatives for their organizations.

One easy example is watching what plays out in politics today. There are numerous instances of Presidential advisors who resign their posts, as stated by the news media. For example, in June 2020, *The Washington Post* reported that a "top state department official resigns in protest ..." when Assistant Secretary of State, Mary Elizabeth Taylor, stepped down from her role. According to the *Post*, which obtained a copy of her resignation letter, this served as, "an indictment of Trump's stewardship at a time of national unrest ..."[4] When you are in disagreement and misalignment with the communication, actions and judgment of your superiors, then the choice to step down is your way of keeping your own values and your integrity intact.

Although we have seen several high-ranking officials leave the Trump administration, this is not solely unique to the Trump White House. Leaving a position in protest happens with all administrations. A quick Google search, at the time of this writing, revealed 14 appointed advisors who left the Obama Administration, although it is not determined if all were in "protest."

An example of stepping down in protest recently played out at Amazon. Vice President Tim Bray resigned because remaining an Amazon VP, for him, would have meant "signing off on actions" that he did not agree with or like. At the time, workers were protesting the conditions of their warehouses during the COVID-19 pandemic. As a result, people were being fired for voicing concerns and showing internal activism. Bray was not going to further what he saw as toxicity filter through the Amazon culture. With his values intact, his choice was to step down.[5]

Of course, we are also seeing plenty of executives step down, unfortunately it is in a response to the way they have handled different situations at their companies. These resignations are less about "do the right thing" moments and are more about the results of not doing the right things in those moments.

Being an ethical leader and role model is knowing your actions send strong signals about who you are and how you want to be remembered.

For all of the aspiring leaders, make your own choices and step down, before you find yourself entangled in the outcome of a "I wish I had done the right thing" moment. If you do not, then you may have someone else steer how you want to live and practice your values, which would be the opposite of who you are and what you really stand for as a person and a professional.

Q82 Should leaders take ethics courses above and beyond what their HR departments require for employee training, based on their stature in a company?

Yes, and here is the reason. Do you remember the movie, *Catch Me If You Can*? It was a film that depicted the life of Frank Abagnale, who was a con man and thief. He forged checks and had the FBI chasing him for years. After spending several years behind bars and serving his prison sentence, Abagnale began working for the government. He wrote his book, *The Art of the Steal*, described on Amazon as "the mind-boggling tricks of the scam trade," and how Abagnale made himself into a sought-after fraud prevention professional.

In 2002, in his reprinted edition, Abagnale mentions the lack of ethics in society. He shares how the unethical used to be the hardened criminals. However, now people who you consider trustworthy do not have the ethics and values that you would expect from them. He even went on to say that the sharp slippage in ethics is what has given rise to a society of fraud. One of the examples he shares in the book is how the popular *Who's Who* reference publication has an edition for *Who's Who Among American High School Students*.

Out of the 16,000 students who were chosen and who filled out a questionnaire, 80% of them answered "Yes" to the following question: During the last three years of high school did you steal, cheat, lie or plagiarize? Abagnale discusses how ethics is taught far too late in the learning process. Thus, the teaching and learning of ethics in school should begin in fifth grade. Since 2002, I don't think ethics classes have been added to elementary and/or middle schools let along high school.[6]

As Abagnale states, if we are living in a society of fraud, then one remedy or positive action step forward would be to teach ethics earlier and more frequently. I would also add that reaching the executive level means more ethical business and communications training. Leaders have a responsibility to lead, which also translates into upholding values and making decisions based on ethical principles and what is good for the people they serve. Of course, you could question how leaders even get to the top if ethics and values were not their guiding compass.

With companies focused on generating ethics policies and training, adding advisory boards and ethics hotlines, and having open discussions with managers and their teams, then what is one more training step for leaders? Taking an extra step, for an ounce of prevention, to advocate leadership ethics certification or continued learning is certainly worth the investment. The goal is to prevent some of the missteps we have seen in corporations and our even our government agencies today.

Even if you do not agree with Frank Abagnale's assessment regarding ethics and society, we can recognize that teaching ethics earlier and more frequently can only help younger generations be more ethics focused in their decision-making as they grow into the leaders of the future.

Q83 What are some of the current pressing topics for leaders who want to be trained in ethical communication?

Bravo to the leaders who want to be trained in the pressing ethical topics playing out in their company communications today. Becoming aware, taking an interest and training to do better as a leader is more than checking off a box to say, "We did this." Instead, the willingness to explore, learn, embrace, and then educate and practice with others through action are bigger steps toward real progress.

I have recently joined the faculty of the Executive Institute on Inclusion (EII), which is an organization created with more than 50 faculty members who have backgrounds in legal affairs, human resources, business management, communications and other professional practices. The faculty was enlisted to instruct and offer workshops on some of the subjects, which are critical topics in business today. There is a real challenge for companies that do not take action to highlight and educate on diversity, equity, inclusion, and racism. EII partners with organizations to create equity and fairness and to work in partnership to create and implement long-term programs. With a mission to overcome what is often systemic in organizations, tough topics are challenged, a new roadmap is carved, and willing executives are behind the charge.[7]

As for the most pressing topics, according to the Global Benchmark 2019 survey, in the United States, the two most commonly observed areas of misconduct in organizations include abusive behavior and conflicts of interest.[8]

Because this is a global survey it is interesting to note how other countries compared:

- **South Africa.** Abusive behavior, at 37%, is the most common observed misconduct.
- **France.** Abusive behavior, at 26%, is the most common observed misconduct.
- **Germany.** Violations of health and/or safety regulations, at 25%, are the most common observed misconduct.

- **United Kingdom.** Abusive behavior, at 29%, is the most common observed misconduct.
- **China.** Corruption, at 23%, is the most common observed misconduct.

Leaders are not only looking at the systemic issues within in their own organizations but also understanding the implications of business with partners around the world.[9]

You have to carry your ethical values in all partner communication and your business transactions. The leaders who are willing to dive deeper—to explore, uncover, understand and take the appropriate action steps to get others to commit to fair practices from a place of integrity, equality and a "do no harm platform"—will move far past the box-checking to the action-driven systems. They will create ethical business standards to lead across teams, generations, and countries.

Q84 How does the company rebound after unethical leadership?

Action and moving beyond "lip service" are the only course forward when a company finds itself having to rebound after unethical leaders fall from grace. The saying, "actions speak louder than words," rings true here. There are any number of examples of companies that have faced severe ethical conduct issues and even legal and criminal charges that set out on a new path to servant leadership and the "do no harm" mantra. They move forward with the fresh leadership, and new systems, and processes in place to prevent what caused the breakdown of ethical judgment in the first place.

The first rebound step is to remove the leader or leaders in charge. According to the 2018 CEO Success Study by Strategy&,[10] more CEOs were released from their duties due to ethical misconduct compared with financial misconduct, in years past. Releasing leaders is a bold step and a necessary one to get an organization back on track after its reputation and possibly bottom line have been affected by poor judgment and unethical behavior.

Other steps to get back on track include being transparent in communication, more internal checks and balances to prevent misconduct from occurring, setting up training systems at regular intervals to help employees understand ethics and how to make better choices based on a company core values. Taking these steps help to show your employees, customers, and the public how you are moving forward with a different mindset; one that is focused on creating fair practices and ethical communication at every touchpoint for the business.

Taking the proper action steps will have your employees and the public be more forgiving in the long term. Any short-term issues that result, need persistent action to resolve. However, it is the long-term plan the leaders create and set in motion that will propel a company further down its path of better judgment.

For the new leaders at the helm, the path is one of transparency, good faith, fair practices and the "do no harm" ethical approach for all in the organization to follow and for which they will be held accountable.

Q85 What do you do if the leaders of the company want to embark on a practice that is unethical or lacks good judgment?

There are times when you will give ethical counsel applying your good judgment. However, this does not always mean the leaders at your company or your clients will agree with your approach or advice.

I have found this is especially true as a communication consultant. There have been times when I have assessed issues for companies and have instructed leaders to be more transparent in their communication. However, they chose to listen to their own instincts and not to listen to a wider perspective in the market.

When I was working with a company (let's call that company "On the Attack"), one of the senior leaders was always ready to pounce on the competition. With his eye closely focused on the number one spot in the market, any action steps to mar or discredit the competition would be a welcomed practice for this leader. He had a "take no prisoners" attitude. It is one thing to watch your competition and to want to outsmart them. Yet, communication goes to a whole new level when you want to take them down publicly and do it any way you can, and quite possibly in an unethical way.

If you are faced with a situation that relates to the competition, let your values guide your ethical behavior. Your competition is still a part of your industry. When they are shown in a negative light and you are ready to bash them and to steel market share, step back and advise your leaders wisely. Today it is your competitor's misstep, tomorrow it could be yours. There are times that uniting around an industry issue or crisis will help you and put you in a better light in the eyes of the public. Any steps to discredit by using inside information to harm or cast the competition in a negative light are unethical.

There will be times, however, that you may have a head-to-head, fair match-up when it comes to your products and theirs. We used to call this the "shootout," when we were doing advertisements or earned media for one of our clients that would show a product's features listed alongside a competitor or a number of competitors. The ad or product review would reveal the many additional features for the price and their advanced technology too. All is fair when it comes to sharing what you have that your competitor does not. However, sharing information that is harmful, inaccurate, or is not representative of the spirit of good competition should be avoided.

The Marketing Experts "Weigh In" on Ethical Guidance

Leaders are Ethical Role Models

By Sheila Murphy, founder and CEO, Focus Forward Consulting

We have all heard the cliché, culture starts at the top, and it is a cliché for a reason—it is right.

How leaders communicate and behave has a tremendous impact on culture, and if they do not model ethical behavior, chances are your organization will suffer. Ethical behavior is not only the right thing to do, it is a smart business decision. What we don't always realize is that what you don't say also matters.

I was speaking to a leader of an organization when he shared with me that one of their business segments was going through a difficult time. The division had not made an ethical choice and was being eaten alive in the press and social media, as well as having their regulators and plaintiffs' counsel beating at their doors. The division was spending a ton of money on crisis managers, attorneys, and consultants to address and remediate the issue. The leader told me that the CEO was shocked that this had happened at his company and was taking aggressive steps to address it. Then the leader turned to me and said:

> "the CEO is a good guy, and he is honestly taken back by what happened, but in all the years he has been our leader, he has spoken 90% of the time on our stock price and financials. I don't recall him talking much about ethics and doing the right thing. I think he thought he didn't have to."

This CEO did not realize that by not discussing ethics, and how employees should behave, he was creating a vacuum where employees would create their own narrative, and that may have been filled in by what they thought he wanted—strong financials and a higher stock price. Leaders set the tone and the guidelines for acceptable behavior. When leadership sets the wrong tone, poor choices can be made, which in this viral work can quickly lead to reputational harm, reduced sales, and flatten stock prices—and perhaps lead to lawsuits and regulatory scrutiny.

In contrast, let's go back to 1982 when someone was killing people by putting cyanide in packages of the nation's leading painkiller, Tylenol. Johnson and Johnson recalled quickly one of its products nationwide—not just where the murders had occurred—and issued warnings not to take the product. Tylenol recovered as a brand and regained its market share, and the world viewed J & J as a company that put people above profits.

Impactful and effective leaders understand the value of ethical behavior to an organization and communicate it consistently. However, it is more critical that the leaders are ethical role models and that by their words and actions, they embody those values regularly. Beyond modeling leaders should explain the thought process behind decisions when ethics are in play. When I was an in-house attorney, it was ingrained that just because we could make a legal argument, that did not mean that we should—and that I needed to understand what was right. As my managers taught me that values, ethics, and doing the right thing mattered, I shared those same lessons with my team.

People need to understand how ethics come into play and how you make those decisions.

Sure, some decisions are "no-brainers," such as not knowingly hiding the potentially lethal side-effects of medication. Other choices are more complex and need inputs from various stakeholders. There can be instances where your company's values may be inconsistent or competing. For example, in a global pandemic, how do you balance individual employees' privacy against the health of other employees. What does a firm do when it has pledged to uplift a community, be environmentally proactive, and grow when it discovers that the new site in which it has invested millions of dollars, and which will bring thousands of promised new jobs and growth, is a breeding ground for an endangered bird. These are not simple answers. You cannot teach someone the right solution for every decision, but you can show them the process they should go through.

Bringing in the various stakeholders to share their perspectives helps a leader understand and appreciate the diverse points of view and the impact on different areas. The leader needs to ask those stakeholders what is the right thing to do and why? The leader is ultimately responsible for the decision, but by understanding and focusing on values, ethics, and the right thing to do, he is in a stronger position to make the right choice.

Leaders have an obligation to themselves, their organization, and their teams to understand their companies' values, to communicate them, and to live them. They will leave their organizations stronger if they model these behaviors and teach their teams how to make ethical decisions.

All Business Activity is Human Activity

By Michael Meath, founder and owner of Fallingbrook Associates, LLC

All business activity is human activity.

This simple yet profound reference, found throughout the book *Business Ethics*,[11] became a key touchpoint for my public relations students at Syracuse University's S.I. Newhouse School of Public Communications over the past several years, as well as my work with CEOs and legal counsel throughout the US as they manage sensitive and crisis situations that include difficult decisions.

I refer to it often and find that it helps leaders of even the most complicated organizations stay on track and true to their mission. It also helps to remind us that a fundamental principle in business ethics is fairness. It always has been, and without it, business would not be able to sustain itself.

Just consider some the most significant ethical breaches in business over the past decade: Wells Fargo, Volkswagen, and Cambridge Analytica. At the end of the day, in each instance, the company's actions came down to human activity and fairness.

Whether we like it or not, organizations look to their leaders as role models for ethical behavior. Employees, customers, suppliers and even competitors watch their actions closely, and it is quite often the little decisions that have the biggest impact on a company's brand or an organization's reputation.

Legal matters are one thing. The law is the law, and we all need to be careful not to rationalize our way around it to fit our unique circumstances. However, there are also lots of scenarios business and organization leaders face outside of legal jurisdiction every day; where the considerations, consequences and obligations associated with a decision could use a bit of structure to help us through the process.

I have learned the hard way that it is not enough to simply rely on my gut instinct. Our "frame," which consists of our social, economic, educational, and religious (or not) background, is all very important. However, we can also benefit from a decision-making process for some of the sensitive matters we face to help us make what Jeffrey Seglin at the Harvard Kennedy School calls "the best right choice."[12]

For me, it all starts with hitting the pause button.

In today's instantaneous-response world powered by a hand-held device it is too easy to fire off a knee-jerk response to a difficult or sensitive question without much thought. However, to make the best right decision, we need just a bit of time to think it through. And, we need some tools that can help us check our instincts. Even as we now try to figure out how to address the growing number of ethical concerns being raised by artificial intelligence, virtual and augmented reality, humans still have a key role to play, even in setting up the technology guardrails for this data driven technology.

Most sensitive and important decisions come down to those made based on cost-vs.-benefit, or consequences (referred to as teleological); and those based on our sense of obligation and duty, regardless of what consequences may follow (deontological). Teleological decisions can be further broken down to those based on the greatest good for the greatest number (utilitarianism), and those based on the best outcome for ourselves or our organization alone (utility).

I know, I know. Many of you are thinking I have gone all John Stuart Mills or Emmanuel Kant on you. But as esoteric as these methods sound (and the important steps that go along with each), we do make better decisions when taking a few minutes to sift through the facts, consider any dominant considerations, and review our decision in a larger context. These methods take practice, but they work. And while it might seem like my decision could ultimately be the same after going through these steps, it gives me some confidence to know I've stopped to consider my place in the world, who else may be impacted, what could occur as a result, and any responsibilities I may have to others.

To put it in practical terms, consider this simple example: A private, closely held business owner has decided she is going to sell her business to an overseas investor later this year. One of the key considerations is the timing of an announcement (to all audiences), since she still has some huge orders to fill under current contractual obligations to her customers. Should she tell her employees now (recognizing that she cannot guarantee their employment after the sale) or hold off a few weeks if the buyer will agree until the large orders are filled? What considerations, consequences and obligations are at play here? Will her decision be based on a cost-vs.-benefit analysis, or sense of duty to her employees, current customers, community, and others?

These are the questions that benefit from the use of a systematic decision-making process.

Company codes of conduct and values statements are important. But they really are not worth the paper they are written on unless leadership sets the tone and provides the example. Remember, everyone is watching you, so you would be well advised to have some of these tools in your box when you get the questions. Traditionalists and baby boomers responded well to "because I said so" statements from their boss; but today's younger generations rightfully question "why" to the decisions an organizational leader makes. So, better to be equipped with the tools to address the questions that will ultimately arise.

We are all human, and we will all make mistakes. I have made some colossal ones. However, wouldn't we make better decisions as organization leaders if we realized that our individual actions have the potential to have a huge impact on the organizations we serve; and that the considerations, consequences and obligations we think about deserve a pause in order to ensure we come up with the best right decision?

I think so ... because all business activity is human activity.

What it Means to be an Ethical Marketer

By Kate Isler, CEO, Author, Board Member, and International Marketing Executive

Ethical (adj.):

1 relating to moral principles or the branch of knowledge dealing with these; morally good or correct. "can a profitable business be ethical?"

The above is a clear and straight forward definition of ethical found in Webster's dictionary. Few leaders would deny that being ethical is table stakes to running a successful business. However, things get tricky when you dig in a bit and start to apply the definitions to real-world situations.

In my career in high-tech business, I have been faced with ethical issues on two fronts. The first, where questions of whether the technology products being developed and positioned to improve people's lives were ethical? Were the improvements being touted morally correct? And did they agree with the cultural norms of ethical behavior?

Second, are the marketing messages used to promote the products ethical? The idea that technology being developed that could make our lives easier is not new. These questions have been around since humans began making better tools to hunt game for food and the wheel to transport it. However, today the dilemma has grown more intense with technologies like Artificial Intelligence (AI) and facial recognition. It is clear that technology can ease parts of life and streamline many tasks, but this convenience comes with a risk of being used to promote undesirable activities. Because these technologies COULD be used in unethical ways, is it ethical to stop innovation?

There is no easy answer. Many have spent long hours debating how the power of innovation will impact human engagement. In my experience, all of this comes down to marketing. Marketing is the critical tool to teach and guide the audience how to incorporate technology into their lives in effective ways. How a product is positioned and sold, to the intended buyer/user is holds the answer to how ethical the product is.

The core of marketing is determining how to talk about what the product does and explaining how it will improve the lives of targeted users. It was this simple exercise that brought me face to face with ethical decisions of marketing.

As with most technology products, marketing is being developed at the same time as the product. The marketing team is given a list of all the product features that they turn into customer benefits. These benefits are used to entice a purchase. But what if the features do not work the way the development team has explained? Can the features still be marketed as benefits to the intended buyer?

I found myself in just that situation while leading a global marketing team for a major technology company. Early leaks about the product touted it as a game-changer. Anticipation was building among enthusiasts and the press coverage about the product being revolutionary, modern and would define the way be people worked across several industries.

The initial demonstrations by the product teams to the marketing community were flawless. The product was beautiful and seamless. We, the marketing team, could not wait to get our hands on it and start developing messages and materials that would get this amazing technology in the hands of users.

A few weeks later, the beta product was handed off to marketing so that my team could start playing with the product and learning the detail of how the technology would deliver on the scenarios we had been developing. It was immediately clear that while the product had worked smoothly when the development team had shared it, in the hands of people less familiar with the product it was hard to use and did not flow the same way.

Realizing the gains that the product promised would require the customer to change the way they interacted with their computer and present a steep learning curve. The leap to a new way of working was too far, and we began to feel as though the claims of "easy to modernize" were overstated.

The marketing team was faced with an ethical decision: Is it ethical to make claims that you know, or feel, are inaccurate to drive sales?

At first glance, the obvious answer is "No". However, executing ethical "No" is not that easy. The pressure to recoup the investment made in the product is high. Momentum and popular opinion inside the organization were in favor of moving ahead with the claims of "easy."

This dilemma took me straight back to the definition of ethical: "relating to moral principles or the branch of knowledge dealing with these." Specifically, the phrase on knowledge dealing with principles.

To be an ethical marketer means finding the balance and the path to creating compelling messages and scenarios that are honest with the audience. This sounds like a heavy lift; however, in reality it comes down to language and function. The marketers' job is to cultivate and secure relationships with customers. Authenticity is table stakes in that relationship.

In the scenario I described, we were able to adjust the language and share the reality that the change required to leverage the new technology fully would be painful; however, in the end, it would be worth it. As a result, we gained loyalty from customers that valued honesty and made the decision to join the journey to achieve the long-term "better" way of working. Those that we lost when we dropped the "easy" stance would have been disappointed and dissatisfied with the product and ultimately could have been more damaging to our brand in the long run.

Ethical Marketing leaders must have and practice vision and be willing to fight for it.

Notes

1 Napolean Hill, *The Law of Success*, 54th edition, The Napolean Hill Foundation, p. 143, 1998.
2 Rick Levine, Christopher Locke, Doc Searls, & David Weinberger, *The Cluetrain Manifesto*, Basic Books; Tenth Anniversary Edition, April 2011.
3 Hélio Garcia, *The Agony of Decision: Mental Readiness and Leadership in a Crisis*, Logos Institute for Crisis Management and Executive Leadership Press, p. 134, July 2017.
4 Seung Min Kim, "Top State Department Official resigns in protest of Trump's response to racial tensions in the country," Washington Post, June 2020.
5 Jason Del Ray, "An Amazon VP's resignation shows internal unrest is rising to the top," Vox Recode, https://www.vox.com/recode/2020/5/4/21246361/amazon-vp-tim-bray-resigns-activist-firing-aws, May 2020.
6 Frank Abagnale, *The Art of the Steal: How to Protect Yourself and Your Business from Fraud*, Currency; Illustrated Edition, November 2002.
7 Executive Institute on Inclusion (EII), Homepage, https://www.executiveinstitut eoninclusion.com, September 2020.
8 ECI Ethics & Compliance Initiative, 2019 Global Benchmark Survey, https://www.ethics.org/knowledge-center/interactive-maps, September 2020.
9 ECI Ethics & Compliance Initiative, 2019 Global Benchmark Survey, Types of Observed Misconduct, https://www.ethics.org/knowledge-center/interactive-map s, September 2020
10 Strategy&, "2018 CEO Success Study: Succeeding the long-serving legend in the corner office," https://www.strategyand.pwc.com/gx/en/insights/ceo-success.htm l, 2019.
11 Richard DeGeorge, *Business Ethics*, Prentice Hall, November 2009.
12 Jeffrey L. Seglin, "Jeffrey Seglin on Ethics for Harvard Business School Publishing, Making the Best Right Choice," YouTube, https://www.youtube.com/wa tch?v=npX3rgTowSc, February 2010.

Chapter 8

Embracing the Ethical Lessons

Ethical Marketers begin their journey with a focus on defining or refining values. However, is there any guarantee these values will align with your company, and mold into the "collective conscience" assembled in your organization? Yes, the potential definitely exists. However, there is a major factor: How your organization, through its leaders, human resources and communications departments and you combined, as the Ethical Marketers, help the process along. Collectively you will need to spell out, with clarity and precision, all the desired behaviors associated with the values you set forth for the company.

In other words, what does good judgment and ethical behavior look like, rather than what do ethics and values sound like? What behaviors should be championed and what actions must be avoided? As an Ethical Marketer, after reading the chapters in this book, you can help to move your organization from thoughts and concepts about ethics, and the accompanying written guidelines, to demonstrating ethical decision-making and good conduct, because you understand how the desired behaviors are shaped daily.

When I was reading the book, *Marilyn: A Woman in Charge*, by author Dick Martin (featured at the end of Chapter 2, "What is Truth?"), I remembered a story Dick shared in his book. In the 1980s, after AT&T was split into several different regional operating companies, Bob Allen, Chief Executive and Chairman at the time, wrote a set of principles called, "Our Common Bond." These principles reflected five important values for all of the company's subsidiaries to uphold. They included respect for individuals, dedication to helping customers, high standards of integrity, innovation, and teamwork. What was interesting to note, from Marilyn Laurie's perspective, was how spelling out the values in words did not always mean the same perceived "good" judgment for all members of the company.[1]

In the book, Marilyn learned of an incident that occurred during a meeting with senior executives. The incident became a lesson of values on paper vs. how actual values were demonstrated through behavior and can be perceived differently. She learned that during the meeting, one executive interrupted the presentation of another executive by yelling, "That's bullshit." Now, if you were a fly on the wall, or not a member of the executive team, or not aware of what "respect for individuals" in the executive culture meant, then you might see this example as the complete opposite of the definition of the word "respect." However, for the executives in the meeting, respect was working out their differences in real-time. They did not believe they had to wait to say something later rather than sharing in the moment. They knew it was important for others at the meeting to see them working out their disagreements, regardless of the words they used. The interaction, was, in fact, still a sign of respect between these two executives.[2]

However, sticking with this example, how would this sign of respect appear to a younger employee who, perhaps, was raised in a family, or a community, or went to a college, where respect meant not interrupting, and respect was not to air your grievances for all to see? How would this play out culturally with global employees. Would there be misalignment? I would say, "Yes." Stating values on a corporate plaque and printing them out in your handbook are simply not enough. You will have many different perspectives and understandings, based on those words alone. Whether you are deemed the Ethical Marketer by the nature of your job, or you are indirectly designated an ethical champion, as a member of your company sharing information through your personal channels, it is the behavior that plays out through your communication that has to be understood and agreed upon.

For all of the organizations taking the time to define or refine their values, there is one more important step. Dive deeper into the actions and identify the desirable behaviors to guide more good judgment. What does this mean and what would those next steps look like in day-to-day terms? As Ethical Marketers, defining the values for the company is only half of the process. As such, you cannot wait and hope for the good judgment to play out on its own. Rather, documenting, rewarding, sharing, and creating awareness through open dialog and ethical resources, you can help other Ethical Marketers stay focused on what appropriate conduct should look like.

However, as you learned in Chapter 2, to get to the good judgment and the ethical behavior, you also have to quickly uncover all of the problem areas. It is not enough to share through training what good communications look like, if you don't expose the issues, solve the problems, and document them for others to learn and avoid. Otherwise, even with good intentions, the journey is far more arduous, and you will experience unnecessary missteps, mismanaged communication and poor judgment, far more than you are prepared to handle.

I am yet to find the perfect marketer or business professional or the perfect business. On the road to personal and professional ethics, mistakes will be made along the way. We are all human and humans are prone to missteps. And there is no utopian business. There are many excellent companies that create impact around the world. Yet, they have their fair share of challenges, issues, and, yes, crises when ethics are seriously in question. Although Sir Thomas More wrote the fictional book, *Utopia*, in 1516, we're still in search of the island where harmony, prosperity and equality would reign with the perfect modernized society void of corruption, crime, and poverty.[3]

It takes an individual, like you, to start the journey to ethics and values, and it happens early in life as your values are being shaped. Then, with good "bumpers" around you, including your parents, friends, extended family, your community and society, educational institutions, and the lessons of life (sometimes even experiencing the School of Hard Knocks), people form their values and continue the molding, as a part of their professional experience. The molding of ethics and values does not stop with one company, or even multiple career changes. If it does, then you would lose your ability to choose what is right, what is good and what fits into the "do no harm" category. If you were to leave your ethics and values at somebody else's door, then you would be giving up your independence and leaving your integrity to chance. However, when you can hold onto your personal choices with certainty, complement your organization and align with others who have like minds and actions, you become a part of the collective conscience. Together, as a team of Ethical Marketers you will make a difference through good judgment efforts and by affecting positive change through your communications as a whole.

Of course, most choices, whether personal or professional, boil down to an important place—where you communicate—with your communication output through many touchpoints. You can define, build, spell out and practice ethics and values repeatedly with your teams and teach the good judgment decision-making. However, getting appropriate behaviors, which demonstrate ethical standards through your channels consistently and in a manner that serves (rather than is self-serving) is how you *practice* marketing ethics. The behaviors playing out and the outcomes that result, are what the public sees, hears, knows, connects with, gravitates to, and allows you to create those strong relationships and unbreakable bonds you seek.

Ethics and values are not "pie in the sky" ideals. They are lived every day, by everyone who wants to be a part of your company. And, on a personal level, anyone who wants to be a part of your world. Even if you are just realizing you are on the road to ethics and values, regardless your age, generation, or what has happened in your past, you are making choices about ethics daily. Make now, your present moment, the "aha!" moment, and a time to look at your decisions as better decisions, especially if some of your choices have had a negative effect on your career and life.

You have traveled a long journey and have made many different choices along the way. With every choice, there is a decision based on your values, and there is also compound effect that plays out as a series of actions and outcomes. I realized the importance of the compound effect after reading best-selling author and self-development professional, Darren Hardy's book. In his book, *The Compound Effect*, it became evident how every decision you make, small or large, has an impact on your life and in business, with more consequences to follow.[4] Sticking to your values and practicing ethical standards are a personal choice and a professional practice revealed through your communications. However, this is not just about your work. The decisions you make on the job are a part of your life choices and vice versa. Whether for business or personal interactions, communication, as Michael Meath mentions in Chapter 7, is a human activity with your values on display.

Start with yourself and then open the door to expanding your beliefs, strengthening your ethics and applying good judgment with the people around you. Remember, you are not just affecting your work environment and the colleagues on your teams. This book started with a look at how values begin in the home and how they are built long before the student enters school. As such, you will also be an ethics role model to your own family, friends, professors, community members, leaders and everyone around you.

Where does the journey to ethics and values take you? To a place with more questions, thoughtful and reflective answers, and a trail of previous decisions and outcomes to use as guidance. Remember, you do not have to make choices alone. Why? Because the choices you make alone are compounded and so are the choices you make with others. So why not gather the broader perspective, experience and knowledge from the people around you, and capitalize together on what truthful, transparent, fair and responsible conduct looks like in those "do the right thing" challenging moments that really matter.

Now, you may be saying, what happens if all the answers offered in the pages to this book still do not reflect a gut choice and the feeling of personal alignment with your company. If this is the case, it is a "do the right thing" moment for yourself. As discussed earlier in the book, sometimes speaking truth to power, when no one else will, means compromising your position at a company. However, it does not mean compromising your own integrity and character. I would rather walk away from a company and a career, than live with something I knew was not a good choice and the mob psychology had prevailed in the worst possible way.

As you move onward and upward, in your career and all your personal choices, you will be tested a lot more. The tests come in many different forms. Having the wisdom of Ethical Marketers helps to guide your decision-making. Afterall, as Michael Meath also shared in Chapter 7, what decision-making approach has helped you? Step back and hit the pause button. Ask yourself if they are deontological or based on a sense of duty or obligation, or teleological which is based on the most good for the most people, or the best outcome, which is utility based. Did you recognize the difference in your decision-making? Perhaps you are now thinking about hitting the pause button more frequently. Whatever knowledge you have learned about your journey to ethics and values and good decision-making, from this point forward, will be your definition of ethics playing out in any number of scenarios.

Keep challenging yourself and testing your own decision-making process. Your goal is to get to the good judgment and ethical behavior so you can watch all the positive compound effects and how they play out in your career and lifetime. Of course, you have an open invitation to ask me questions and to share with me your personal journey and business practice as an Ethical Marketer, whether you are in marketing or any department of your company. If you want to continue the journey and share, then you can find me on Twitter, I'm @dbreakenridge, connect with me on LinkedIn, or you can email me directly at Deirdre@PurePerformanceComm.com.

Be sure to also take up these conversations with your peers and colleagues by joining different professional groups on LinkedIn or by starting your own discussion group in your organization. The topic of ethics is prominent in our society and in your companies. We live in a world where ethics and values are challenged by the second, and you will be tested over and over again. After all, adding to the challenges will be the fast-paced dynamic media landscape, constantly evolving because of technological advances, which do not cease.

Business utopia may be nowhere in sight. However, there is an army of ethical people and champions who surround you looking to form a collective conscience for the good of your company and for the good of society. Minds joining in harmony and cooperation can be powerful together. People who organize have more pull and suggestion than single minds acting alone, unharmoniously, and perhaps unethically, and not in sync with others.

Are you ready to take on the ethical challenges of these times? If you are, then you will be learning, assessing, experiencing the collective thinking, sharing information, and communicating with your ethics and values in the forefront. You will be leading the way with your Ethics GPS.

Good luck on your journey as an Ethical Marketer. As you move along your path, remember there will be others looking to you and up to you. Be sure to encourage the asking of questions and be generous in your answers. You will also want to "walk the ethics talk!" When you do, the personal and professional opportunities will surface and so will your continued, and compounded successes.

Notes

1 Dick Martin, *Marilyn: A Woman in Charge. Marilyn Laurie's Life in Public Relations*, PRMuseum Press, LLC, p. 118, September 2020.
2 Ibid., p. 117.
3 British Library, Thomas More's Utopia 1516, https://www.bl.uk/learning/tim eline/item126618.html, September 2020.
4 Darren Hardy, *The Compound Effect*, Hachette Go, September 2020.

Index

Abagnale, Frank 140–41, 150n6
Abrams, Abigail 92n1
accountability 11, 27, 43, 51, 83, 84; imperative of acceptance of 137; lack of, problem of 29; responsibility and 40
accurate information, spread of 125–8
Activa 99
Advertising Value Equivalents (AVEs) 51–2
advertorials, ethics in 29–30
advocacy, relationships and 24
The Agony of Decision (Garcia, H.) 136, 150n3
Airbnb 83
Allen, Bob 151
"alternative facts" 3
Amazon 140
American Apparel 82
American Marketing Association (AMA) 16, 129
American Society for the Prevention of Cruelty to Animals (ASPCA) 74–6, 76n13–14; Pet Health Insurance 75
amplifiers in social media 58–9
apologies, good practice in making 45
Ariely, Dan 92n3
The Art of the Steal (Abagnale, F.) 140
Arter, Melanie 57n6
Arthur Anderson 109
Arthur W. Page Society 81; Online Knowledge Center 40; Page Principles 123
artificial intelligence (AI) 3, 146, 148
AT&T 54–6; "Our Common Bond," Allen's principles for 151
audience trust, warning against compromise of 75–6
Aunt Jemima Syrup 98

Bistrong, Richard 13, 25n8
bloggers: ethical issues in digital marketing with 32–3; ethical standards for journalists and 39–40
Bloomberg media 83
Bowen, Dr. Shannon 40, 57n15
BP (British Petroleum) 83
Bradley, Diana 57n8
brands: brand policing 26; brand values, personal and partners' consistency in 75; engagement with causes, downsides of 58–9; false claims and misleading information about 31; mistakes with, dealing through media with upset customers 83; non-profits brands, value of 74–5; staying true to your brand in cause marketing 74–6; trusted brands in cause marketing, rationales for 59–60
Bray, Tim 139
Breakenridge, Deirdre K. 25n9, 56n1, 57n19, 155
Brown, M.E. 131n8
Brown, Suzanne 91–2, 108–10
Burger KIng 66–7
Burke, Shonali 74–6, 117–19
business activities: human activity and 145–7; personal vs. professional ethics in communications for 8–9
Business Ethics (DeGeorge, R.) 145–6, 150n11
Business Roundtable 72, 76n6
buying followers on social media, ethical or not? 43–4

Cambridge Analytica 146
campaigning, key components for success in 69
Carnegie, Dale 12, 25n6

Catch Me If You Can? (Steven
  Spielberg film) 140
cause marketing 4, 58–76; audience
  trust, warning against compromise of
  75–6; brand engagement with,
  downsides of 58–9; brand values,
  personal and partners' consistency in
  75; building programs for, rationale
  for 67–8; campaign for, key
  components for success in 69; causes
  to support, choice of 68–9, 72;
  charitable partners, functional
  responsibilities of 65–6; choices,
  alignment with causes,
  decision-making on 58, 67–8, 72;
  communication judgment, dealing
  with deficiencies in 63–4; definition
  of 59–60; "Do Well by Doing Good"
  59; employee branding surveys 68;
  ethical approaches, brands giving
  and taking 69; ethical challenges in
  programs of, reasons for building in
  spite of 67–8; Ethical Marketers,
  cause marketing initiative for 59;
  Ethical Marketers, change
  management for 64–5; Ethical
  Marketers, responsibilities as
  partners in 65; ethical missteps in,
  creation of change for prevention of
  64–5; ethics in 71–3; ethics in,
  resources for learning about 62–3;
  ethics in, use of 58–76; ethics in
  communication, team education for
  65–6; greenwashing, ethical perils of
  72; mistakes in programs, avoidance
  in 73; mistakes in programs, dealing
  with 61–2; problem areas to avoid in
  60–61; public backlash against
  campaigns 66–7; ramping up
  program, team education for ethics
  in communication 65–6; staying true
  to your brand in 74–6; top issues
  with 72–3; transparency, best
  approach in 61–2; trusted brands in,
  rationales for 59–60; unethical cause
  marketing 70–71; vagueness of
  claims, problem of 73; value of
  non-profits brands 74–5; win-win
  possibilities in 70–71
C+C in Boston 71–2, 128–9
Centers for Disease Control and
  Prevention (CDC) 85

charitable partners, functional
  responsibilities of 65–6
choices: alignment with causes,
  decision-making on 58, 67–8, 72;
  causes to support in cause marketing,
  choice of 68–9, 72; judgment,
  decision-making and 153–4; lying,
  problem of 10–11; mentors, common
  traits to look for in choice of 114;
  unethical decisions, speaking up
  about 12–13; wrongdoing and
  shifting blame for 11–12; *see also*
  decision-making
Clinton, Hillary 85
Clorox 31
The Cluetrain Manifesto (Levine, R. et
  al.) 135, 150n2
"collective conscience" of organizations
  94, 155
communication: accuracy in 7, 12, 17;
  auditing of, exercise in 17–18;
  blocking of good judgment in 26–7;
  building trust in 135–6; challenges in,
  mentee questions about 117–19;
  company reputations and lack of
  ethics in 96–7; confidential
  information, ethical dealing with
  50–51; consumer information about
  data privacy and security,
  dissemination of 36–7; crisis
  management and 82; dealing with
  poor judgment in 104–5;
  decision-making and ethics in process
  of 26–7; ethical behavior, exposure in
  8; ethics and values in daily
  interactions 7; inter-corporate flows
  17; judgment about, dealing with
  deficiencies in 63–4; landscape of,
  radical change in 3; mailing lists, use
  on those not 'opted in' for receipt of
  information 38–9; marketing ethics
  in, practice of 153; marketing
  "problem areas" and unethical
  communications 17–18; media
  channels, application of ethics
  through 53–4; personal *vs.*
  professional ethics in
  communications for business 8–9;
  prevention of poor judgment in
  103–4; responsibility for unethical
  communications 15–16; signposts to
  ethical communications 20–21; social

media participation, good judgment considerations for 40–41; training for leaders in ethical communications 141–2; transparency in 1; truth in 54–6; unethical decisions, challenging before sharing 13–14; values and ethics in 94; values on display in 154
Answers for Modern Communicators (Breakenridge, D.K.) 15, 59, 62–3
The Compound Effect (Hardy, D.) 154, 155n4
Conference Board/Ernst & Young Global Leadership Forecast 72
confidentiality: accidental breach of confidential information, dealing with 50–51; with competitive information 99
consumer information about data privacy and security, dissemination of 36–7
corporate social responsibility (CSR) 58, 63
Covid-19 pandemic 31, 57n7, 59, 69, 72, 76n2, 82, 88, 139
Crane, Jim 115
crisis situations 53, 54, 96, 97–8, 120–21, 143, 146; emotional intelligence (EI) in 10; Golden Hour of Crisis Response 136–7; management and communication in 50, 82; reputation management in 26; self-promotion in 58–9
crowdsourcing 16
customer experience (CX) 101–2

Dade County, Hurricane Andrew devastation in (1992) 90
Daily, Matt 93n13
Dale, Daniel 131n6
Dalfonzo, Stephanie 90–91
D'Angelo, Anthony 121–4
Dannon 99
data collection 36
data privacy, technology and 99
Davis, Scott 131n5
decision-making: challenging and testing approaches to 155; ethical decision-making, seeking guidance on 100–101; ethics in 2; and ethics in process of communication 26–7; good judgment in 134; missteps in 1; policy repository, ethical

decision-making and 100; spreading ethical decision-making among peers 14; unethical decisions, speaking up about 12–13, 21; *see also* choices
Del Ray, Jason 150n5
Deloitte Global Millennial Survey 58, 75n1
Dietrich, Arment 52–3, 124–5
Dietrich, Gini 52–3, 56n2, 124–5
digital advertising: changes of ethics in 28–9; transparency in 31–2
digital marketing: ethical issues with bloggers in 32–3; practices leading to search engine bans 37–8; privacy issues in 35–6; responsibility for ethics in 34–5; systemic breakdown, dealing with 35
DISC Profile test 134
discrimination in communications 98–9
dishonesty 79
Disinformation Age 73
disinformation and misinformation, difference between 84–5
Douglas, Danielle 93n12
Dupixent, disclaimers about negative side effects 30
Duracell 82

Edelman, Richard 71, 76n5
Edelman Trust Barometer 18–19, 71, 76n5, 116
Ellis, Colin D. 131n3
Ellison, Sarah 131n7
emotional intelligence (EI): definition of 10; ethical behavior and 9–10; guidance from 24–5; personal level of, evaluation of 10
emotional quotient (EQ) 137
empathy: earning of, hard work in 122; empathetic communication 120; fan empathy 62; kindness, respect and, need for 23; understanding and, need for 136
employee branding surveys 68
Engineering and Technology, Institute of 42
Enron 109
environmental influences on professional ethics 7–8, 10–11
ethical behavior 2, 5–6, 7, 26, 27, 95, 109–10, 126, 143; cultural norms of 148; demonstration of 78; emotional

intelligence (EI) and 9–10; exposure in communication 8; four pillars of ethics and 115; good judgment and 151, 152–3; integrity and 23; litmus test for 20; modelling of 106, 144–6; organizational values and 97; standard of 3–4; transparency and 88

ethical challenges: in programs of, reasons for building in spite of 67–8; stepping down in protest at 139–40

ethical champions in companies, development of 106

ethical choices *see* choices; decision-making

ethical conduct, demonstrations of 134

ethical guidance, personal and professional values and 52–3

ethical issues, common problems in organizations and occurrence of 98–9

Ethical Marketers: advertorials, top tips for 29–30; amplification of ethical communication in interviews 78; bloggers, screening for unethical behavior 32–3; brand communications for 65; cause marketing initiative for 59; celebrities, awareness of dangers of claims of 31; change management for 64–5; characteristics of 2–4; charitable organizations, communications for 65–6; consumer information, precautions with 36–7; decision-making and good judgment of 3–4; decision-making approaches of 154–5; ethics in marketing 148–9; human resources (HR) function and 94–5; inauthentic bots, dealing with 42; interviewing for 78; organizational penetration by, media effectiveness and 26–8; practice of good judgment and 32; responsibilities as partners in cause marketing 65; sharing experiences 5; social media participation, good judgment considerations for 40–41; Standard Operating Procedure (SOP) for 47; truth in public relations (PR), practical application of 55–6; values, definition and refining of 5–6, 151–2

ethical minds, training for 128–9

ethical missteps: creation of change for prevention of 64–5; on social media, dealing with 44–5

ethical role models: leaders as 144–5; meaning of 137–8

ethical testing, company requirement for 105

ethics: advice from a mentors on 120–21; cause marketing, use of ethics in 58–76; Codes of Ethical Conduct 16–17; in communication, team education for 65–6; courses for leaders in 140–41; "do no harm," principle of 2, 20, 31, 40, 81, 138, 142–3, 153; ethical behavior, ongoing conversation about 5–6; ethical standards, definition of 3; Ethics 101 Manual 11; ethics advice 19; Ethics GPS 5, 8–9, 14, 19, 25n1, 78, 155; ethics hotline, ethical decision-making and 101; ethics oversight board, ethical decision-making and 101; Four Pillars of (Trust, Honesty, Transparency, and Responsibility) 115–16; guidance for personal and professional ethics implementation 16–17; higher education and reinforcement of 8–9; judgment and 4; learning about ethics in cause marketing, resources for 62–3; media interviews and 88–90; organizational actions in violation of ethical values 126–7; for organizations, finding out about 97–8; practice of 3; in social media, responsibility for 43; standards for leaders 138–9; true freedom and 90–91; values and, lived ideals 153; values and, moulding of 153–5; values in daily interactions and 7

ethics in organizations 4–5, 94–110; "collective conscience" and 94, 155; communication, company reputations and lack of ethics in 96–7; communication, dealing with poor judgment in 104–5; communication, prevention of poor judgment in 103–4; communication, values and ethics in 94; confidentiality with competitive information 99; customer experience

(CX) 101–2; data privacy, technology and 99; discrimination in communications 98–9; ethical champions in companies, development of 106; ethical decision-making, seeking guidance on 100–101; ethical issues, common problems in organizations and occurrence of 98–9; ethical organizations, steering towards 108–10; ethical testing, company requirement for 105; ethics for organizations, finding out about 97–8; ethics hotline, ethical decision-making and 101; ethics oversight board, ethical decision-making and 101; filtering ethics through organizations 95; harassment in communications 98–9; information, external sharing of 99–100; judgment, dealing with poor judgment in communication 104–5; legal department, ethical decision-making and 101; lying to customers 99; marketing, four Ps in (product, promotion, price and place) 102; misrepresentation of services 99; numbers, misrepresentation of 98; origins of ethics in companies? 95–6; policy repository, ethical decision-making and 100; public relations (PR), marketing, sales and customer service, intersection of ethics between 101–2; racism in communications 98–9; risk management, ethical decision-making and 101; society and ourselves, ethical obligations to 106–8; talent office, ethical decision-making and 100; team building 103–4; technology and data privacy 99; trust, activities for building 103–4; trust, effects of breakdowns of 96–7
European Union (EU) 33–4
exaggeration or lying in media interviews 80–81
Executive Institute on Inclusion (EII) 141; mentoring, ethics and 112–14
expectations, leadership and 138
expert interview status 77

Facebook 16, 83, 87–8; Facebook Pixel 35
Fach, Melissa 57n21
facial recognition technology 148
FactCheck.org 49
Fairleigh Dickinson University Global Business Management (GBM) program 103
"fake news" 3; challenge of? 49–50
Fallingbrook Associates, LLC 145–7
Fauci, Dr. Anthony 85, 93n16
Federal Bureau of Investigation (FBI) 13, 140
Federal Trade Commission (FTC) 32
FIFA World Cup 62
filtering ethics through organizations 94–110
Fletcher, Michael 93n12
Florida Public Relations Association 13
Floyd, George 97, 98–9
Focus Forward Consulting 144–5
Ford Motors 48
Fox, Vanessa 57n11
Fox News 30–31
Freberg, Karen 129–31
Freeman, Susan 112–14
Frito-Lay 69
Front-Line Anti-Bribery LLC. 13

Garcia, Hélio ('Fred') 136, 150n3
Garrett, Neil 92n3
General Data Protection Regulation (GDPR) in EU 33–4
Generation Z (Gen Zers) 12
genetic testing 108
Gentile, Mary 113, 131n2
"Giving Voice to Values" (Gentile, M.) 113
Glavin, Wendy 23–5
Glazer, Emily 25n5
Global Alliance, Global Principles of Ethics for 123
Global Benchmark 2019 survey 141–2
Golcher, Holly 70–71
Golden Hour of Crisis Response 136–7
Goodbye Anxiety, Hello Freedom (Dalfonzo, S.) 90–91
Google 16, 37, 63, 73, 80; Search Engine Optimization (SEO) Starter Guide 38
Grant, Adam 24, 25n15
greenwashing, ethical perils of 72
Gunia, Brian C. 132n12

Hannity, Sean 30–31
harassment in communications
98–9
Hardy, Darren 153–4, 155n4
Harrison, D.A. 131n8
Harvard Kennedy School 146
Harwood, John 25n13
'Haste Makes Waste' on social media
49
Hathaway, Anne 126
Haylett, Corie 93n7
Hayward, Tony 84
Heilpern, Will 110n2
Hill, Napoleon 133, 150n1
Hippocrates 20
Ho, Erica 93n8
honesty 90, 112, 138, 149; core value of
118, 119; ethics pillar of 115–16
Honeysett, Alex 93n14
Horsley, Scott 25n7
Houston Astros 115
How to Stop Worrying and Start Living
(Carnegie, D.) 12
Howard, Jacqueline 131n6
Hurricane Sandy in New England
(2012) 82

IBM 48
Iliff, Rebekah 20–21
*I'm Very Ferris: A Child's Story about
in Vitro Fertilization* (Kossow, T.)
108
information: accurate information,
mentoring and spread of 125–8;
consumer information about data
privacy and security, dissemination
of 36–7; delivery of, accuracy in 8,
81–2, 88; external sharing of
99–100
in vitro fertilization (IVF) 107–8
Insider 82
Instagram 33
integrity 3–4, 7, 18, 20, 24, 67, 81, 112,
134, 142, 151; asset of 22–3, 139;
business integrity 91–2; character and
26, 51, 138, 154; credibility and 28;
ethical organizations, integrity in
108–9, 110; in media interviews and
appearances 92
intelligence quotient (IQ) 137
inter-corporate flows of communication
17

International Association of Business
Communicators (IABC)
16–17
International Risk Management
Institute (IRMI) 110n3
Internet 4, 21; speed of 26; unethical
behavior on 27; *see also* social media
27
interview preparation 78
Isler, Kate 148–9

Jackson, Pat 122
Jacobs, Ken 125–8
Jacobs Consulting & Executive
Coaching 125–8
JCPenney 38
Joel, Billy 116
Johnson, Ted 57n7
Johnson & Johnson 144
journalists, ethical standards for
bloggers and 39–40
judgment: communication, blocking of
good judgment in 26–7;
communication, dealing with poor
judgment in 104–5; emotional
intelligence (EI) and 9–10; Ethical
Marketers, practice of good
judgment and 32; fostering good
judgment in decision-making 133;
good judgment 13, 14, 27–8, 31, 38,
49; good judgment, cause marketing
initiatives and 59; good judgment,
characteristics of 40–41; good
judgment, ethics in decision-making
and 2–3, 4–5, 35, 94; good sense and
wise judgment 77; listening without
7; missteps and poor judgment 43,
58; negative outcomes, poor
judgment and 11; organizations
lacking good judgment, working
with 63–4; poor judgment 15, 19, 27,
29, 31, 39, 61, 62, 63; poor judgment,
demonstrations of 44, 47; poor
judgment, unethical decision-making
and 4, 58; rectification of poor
judgment 35; self-serving messages,
poor judgment in 81–2; social media,
good judgment considerations for
communication on 40–41; standards,
good judgment and improvement in
9, 19; teaching good judgment,
recognition of bad behavior and 48

Kant, Immanuel 147
Karma school of business 20–21
Knight, Bernard 25n2
Knight, Will 57n18
Kossow, Tess 106–8
Kouzes, J.M. 131n1

Laurie, Marilyn 151–2
The Law of Success (Hill, N.) 133, 150n1
Lazzaro, Stephanie 92n3
leadership and ethics 5, 133–49; accountability, imperative of acceptance of 137; *The Agony of Decision* (Garcia, H.) 136, 150n3; *The Art of the Steal* (Abagnale, F.) 140; business activities, human activity and 145–7; *Business Ethics* (DeGeorge, R.) 145–6, 150n11; *Catch Me If You Can?* (Steven Spielberg film) 140; *The Cluetrain Manifesto* (Levine, R. et al.) 135, 150n2; communication, building trust in 135–6; communication, training for leaders in ethical communications 141–2; decision-making, good judgment in 134; DISC Profile test 134; ethical challenges, stepping down in protest at 139–40; ethical conduct, demonstrations of 134; Ethical Marketer, meaning of 148–9; ethical role models, leaders as 144–5; ethical role models, meaning of 137–8; ethical standards for leaders 138–9; ethics courses for leaders 140–41; expectations, leadership and 138; Golden Hour of Crisis Response 136; *The Law of Success* (Hill, N.) 133, 150n1; leaders, ethical standards for 138–9; leaders, ethics courses for 140–41; leadership skills 133–4; listening and leadership 19; Myers and Briggs Personality Types test 134; sharing ethically challenging situations, dilemma of 136–7; StrengthsFinder 134; training for leaders in ethical communications 141–2; transparency, imperative of 23, 136, 137; trust building, leadership and 135–6; unethical leadership, effects of 142–3; unethical practices by senior management,

dealing with 143; visionary leadership 133
The Leadership Challenge (Kouzes, J. M. & Posner, B.Z.) 113
learning about ethics: beginnings of 7; by example, mentoring and 112–14
legal department, ethical decision-making and 101
Lepitak, Stephen 76n3
Levine, Rick 135, 150n2
LinkedIn 16, 37, 62, 155
Locke, Christopher 135, 150n2
Louisville, University of 129–31
Lululemon 83
lying: misrepresentation and lying to customers 99; problem of 10–11, 20, 81

mailing lists, use on those not 'opted in' for receipt of information 38–9
Major League Baseball (MLB) 34, 115
Manea, Corina 22–3
Marilyn: A Woman in Charge (Martin, D.) 151–2, 155n1–2
marketing: bloggers, ethical issues in digital marketing with 32–3; digital footprints and 35–6; "dos" and "don'ts" of data protection for advertising and 34; ethics in, practice of 153; ethics in marketing 148–9; false claims in 30–31; four Ps in (product, promotion, price and place) in 102; media channels and 4, 26–56; paying for good stories, violation of ethical principles in 56; "problem areas" and unethical communications 17–18; programs for, GDPR and ethics in 33–4; purchased followers, signs of 44; technology, introduction through 148–9; *see also* digital marketing; Ethical Marketers
Martin, Dick 54–6, 151, 155n1–2
Martin Waxman Communications 53–4, 120–21
Marx, Groucho 122
MasterCard 62
McClennan, Mark W. 71–3, 128–9
McCormick, Gary 122
McMaster University 120
Meath, Michael 120–21, 145–7, 154
media agendas, prediction of 77

media channels, application of ethics through 53–4
media interviews and appearances 77–92; brand mistakes, dealing through media with upset customers 83; crisis management 82; disinformation and misinformation, difference between 84–5; Ethical Marketers, amplification of ethical communication in interviews 78; ethics, media interviews and 88–90; ethics, true freedom and 90–91; exaggeration or lying in media interviews 80–81; expert interview status 77; goal of participation in 77; integrity in 92; interview preparation 78; media agendas, prediction of 77; misinformation and disinformation, difference between 84–5; missteps by organizations or leaders, dealing with 83–4; mistakes in interviews, dealing with 81; number inflation in media interviews 79–80; questions to which you don't know answers, dealing with 86; self-serving messages in crisis situations 81–2; transparency, ethical behavior and 88; transparency, sharing information and 87–8; trust and truth 91–2; trusting media with identity "off the record" 86–7; truth, white lies and steering away from 79
Mental Health Awareness 66
mentoring and ethics 5, 111–31; accurate information, asking mentors to help spread it for you 125–8; allegations of unethical behavior, investigation of 127; choice of mentor, common traits to look for 114; communication challenges, mentee questions about 117–19; ethical mentoring, sharing experiences of 121–4; ethical minds, training for 128–9; ethical values, organizational actions in violation of 126–7; ethics advice from a mentor, best of? 120–21; Executive Institute on Inclusion (EII) 112–14; "Giving Voice to Values" (Gentile, M.) 113; honesty, ethics pillar of 115–16; *The Leadership Challenge* (Kouzes, J.M. & Posner, B.Z.) 113; learning ethics by example 112–14; mentee questions, examples of 117–19; mentors 111; mentors, ethics education and 111–12; mentors, questions for discussion with 127–8; mentorship for rising professionals 129–31; organizational actions, interpretation of 126; questions you can ask of mentors 124–5, 125–8; responsibility, ethics pillar of 115, 116–17; responsible mentorship, ethics of 115–17; training the ethical mind 128–9; transparency, ethics pillar of 115, 116; trust, ethics pillar of 115, 116; unethical situations, asking mentors to help in clean up of 125–8
Messi, Lionel 62
Mill, John Stuart 147
Milligan, Amanda 76n4
misinformation: disinformation and, difference between 84–5; effects of sharing 13, 15; misleading information, honest mistakes and 2; services, misrepresentation of 99; spotting bots on social media to avoid sharing 41–2
missteps: mistakes and 152–3; by organizations or leaders, dealing with 83–4
mistakes: in cause marketing programs, avoidance in 73; in cause marketing programs, dealing with 61–2; in interviews, dealing with 81
Mollica, Jason 115–17
Moore, Thomas 76n5
More, Sir Thomas 153, 155n3
Morgan, Blake 93n11
Moynihan, Senator Daniel P. 54
MSNBC 11th Hour 80
Murphy, Sheila 144–5
Myers and Briggs Personality Types test 134

National Alliance on Mental Illness (NAMI) 66
National Institute of Health (NIH) 85
National Library Association 40
National Mall in Washington, DC 79
Nationwide Veterinary Pet Insurance 74
Nature Neuroscience 79
NBC Nightly News 80

New York City subways 12
New York Times 21, 38
Neymar 62
9/11 terrorist attack 9, 54
Noor, Iqra 57n13
numbers: misrepresentation of, ethics in organizations and 98; number inflation in media interviews 79–80

o.b. Tampons 83
Obama, President Barack (and administration of) 79, 139
Oreo and "You Can Still Dunk in the Dark" at Super Bowl XLVII 29
organizational actions, interpretation of 126
Originals: How Non-Conformists Move the World (Grant, A.) 24
origins of ethics in companies? 95–6
Öz ("Dr. Oz"), Dr. Mehmet Cengiz 30–31

Panera Bread 32
personal ethics: challenges to 9; grandparents'; spectrum of disappointment 21; guidance for personal and professional ethics implementation 16–17; lying and dealing with 10–11; personal *vs.* professional ethics 8–9
Personal Protective Equipment (PPE) 88
PESO model (Paid, Earned, Shared and Owned) media 27
Playboy Magazine 21
policy repository, ethical decision-making and 100
Politifact.com 49
Pontefract Group 76n7
Posner, B.Z. 131n1
power, speaking truth to 15–16, 62–3, 154
professional ethics 2–3; accidental breach of confidential information, dealing with 50–51; advertorials, ethics in 29–30; apologies, good practice in making 45; data collection and 36; deletion or hiding posts on social media, ethicality of avoiding brand damage by 46; digital advertising, changes of ethics in

28–9; digital advertising, transparency in 31–2; digital marketing, ethical issues with bloggers in 32–3; digital marketing, practices leading to search engine bans 37–8; digital marketing, privacy issues in 35–6; digital marketing, responsibility for ethics in 34–5; digital marketing, systemic breakdown, dealing with 35; environmental influences on 7–8, 10–11; ethical guidance, personal and professional values and 52–3; Ethics 101 Manual 11; "fake news," challenge of? 49–50; guidance for personal and professional ethics implementation 16–17; Karma school of business 20–21; learning about, beginnings of 7; mailing lists, use on those not 'opted in' for receipt of information 38–9; marketing, false claims in 30–31; measurement of public relations (PR) results based on older values, ethicality of 51–2; media channels, application of ethics through 53–4; misinformation, spotting bots on social media to avoid sharing 41–2; personal *vs.* professional ethics 8–9; social media participation, code of ethics for 40–41; truth and 54–6
PRSA (Public Relations Society of America) 63, 122, 127, 129, 132n11; Code of Ethics of 16, 118–19, 123, 132n11; Ethics and Social Media Advisory 40
Pryor, Greg 132n10
public relations (PR): ethical issues and 18–19; marketing, sales and customer service, intersection of ethics between 101–2; measurement of results based on older values 51–2
The Practice of Public Relations (Seitel, F.) 10–11
Public Relations Society of America, Code of Ethics of 118–19, 123
'Publisher Matters' on social media 49
purchase of followers on social media, ethical or not? 43–4
Putting the Public Back in Public Relations (Breakenridge, D.K. and Solis B.) 13

Quaker Oats 98
Quantas 73
questions: to which you don't know
    answers, dealing with 86; you can
    ask of mentors 124–5, 125–8
'Quotes and More' on social media
    50

racism in communications 98–9
Raymond, Adam K. 25n4
reflectiveness 24–5, 78, 121, 154
reporting unethical behavior on social
    media 48–9
respect: different perceptions of 151–2;
    kindness and, paramount nature for
    ethical behavior 23
responsibility: ethics pillar of 115,
    116–17; responsible mentorship,
    ethics of 115–17
'Reverse the Search' on social media 50
Rexrode, Christina 25n5
risk management, ethical
    decision-making and 101
Robb, Amanda 93n17
Roig-Franzia, Manuel 131n7
Rolling Stone magazine 85
Rosmarin, Remi 93n6

safety, rapid reaction to issue of 1
search engines, practices banned from
    37–8
Searls, David ('Doc') 135, 150n2
Securities and Exchange Commission
    (SEC) 109
Seglin, Jeffrey I. 146
Seitel, Fraser 10–11, 25n3
self-serving messages in crisis situations
    81–2
Seung Min Kim 150n4
sharing ethically challenging situations,
    dilemma of 136–7
Sharot, Tali 92n3
Shonali Burke Consulting, Inc. 74–6,
    117–19
social media: amplifiers in 58–9; buying
    followers on, ethical or not? 43–4;
    deletion or hiding posts on, ethicality
    of avoiding brand damage by 46;
    engagement on, value alignment and
    necessity for 47–8; ethical missteps
    on, dealing with 44–5; ethics in,
    responsibility for 43; 'Haste Makes

Waste' on 49; misinformation,
    spotting bots to avoid sharing 41–2;
    participation in, code of ethics for
    40–41; posts on, ethicality of hiding
    or deleting 46; 'Publisher Matters' on
    49; 'Quotes and More' on 50;
    reporting unethical behavior on 48–9;
    'Reverse the Search' on 50; 'Social
    Media Cases to Distill Ethical
    Guidelines' (Bowen, S.) 40, 57n15;
    speed of 26; trolling, dealing with
    46–7; "trolls" on, dealing with 46–7;
    'URL Says a Lot' on 49–50
society and ourselves, ethical
    obligations to 106–8
Society of Human Resource
    Management (SHRM) 80
Spencer, Saranac Hale 93n16
Spicer, Sean 79
Spin Sucks 52–3, 124–5
Strategic Communications, Online
    Master's Degree Program in
    (American University) 115–17
Strategy & 2018 CEO Success Study
    142, 150n10
Strauss, Karsten 76n10
Streep, Meryl 126
StrengthsFinder 134
Subject Matter Experts (SMEs) 86,
    117–18
Sun, Winnie 88–90
Sun Group Wealth Partners 88–90
Syracuse University, S.I. Newhouse
    School of Communication at 120,
    121–4

talent office, ethical decision-making
    and 100
Taylor, Mary Elizabeth 139
team building in organizations 103–4
technology, data privacy and 99
Toms 59–60, 76n2
Toyota 83
training: the ethical mind 128–9; for
    leaders in ethical communications
    141–2
Transocean Limited 83
transparency 2, 8, 17, 36, 43, 65, 69;
    accidental breach of confidential
    information, dealing with 50–51; best
    approach in cause marketing 61–2; in
    communication 1, 77, 96, 135–6; in

digital advertising 31–2; digital
advertising, transparency in 31–2;
ethical behavior and 88; ethics pillar
of 115, 116; imperative of, leadership
and 23, 136, 137; information
delivery with 81–2; lack of, problem
of 60, 96, 99; sharing information
and 87–8; in social media
communities, rewards for 46; trust
building and 103, 135–6
Trevino, L.K. 131n8
trolling, dealing with 46–7
Trump, President Donald J. 31, 45, 79,
115, 131n7, 139
trust: activities for building 103–4;
building of, leadership and 135–6;
effects of breakdowns of 96–7; ethics
pillar of 115, 116; transparency and
building of 103, 135–6; trusted
brands in cause marketing, rationales
for 59–60; trusting media with
identity "off the record" 86–7; truth
and, media appearances and 91–2
truth: in communication, essential of
54–6; professional ethics and 54–6;
white lies and steering away from 79
Twitter 16, 46–7, 63, 66, 87–8, 155
Tylenol 144

Uber 34
Underwriters Laboratories (UL) 72
unethical behavior: investigation of
allegations of 127; screening bloggers
for 32–3
unethical cause marketing 70–71
unethical communications: marketing
"problem areas" and 17–18;
responsibility for 15–16
unethical decision-making, poor
judgment and 4, 58
unethical leadership, effects of 142–3
unethical practices by senior
management, dealing with 143
unethical situations, asking mentors to
help in clean up of 125–8
United Nations World Food
Programme (WFP) 62

University of Southern California (USC)
72, 76n8
'URL Says a Lot' on social media 49–50
Utopia (More, T.) 153, 155n3

Valinsky, Jordan 110n1
values: brand values, personal and
partners' consistency in 75;
communications, values and ethics in
94; communications, values on
display in 154; defining character of
ethics and 23–5; definition and
refining of 5–6, 7–8, 151–2; on
display in communications 154;
ethical guidance, personal and
professional values and 52–3; ethics
and, lived ideals 153; ethics and
values in daily interactions 7;
everyday MO (Modus Operandi) and
7; "Giving Voice to Values" (Gentile,
M.) 113; organizational values and
ethical behavior 97
Vigdor, Neil 131n4
virtual Town Hall meetings 97–8
visionary leadership 133
Volkswagen 146

Walgreens 48
Walmart 48
The Washington Post 139
Waxman, Martin 53–4, 120–21
Weinberger, David 135, 150n2
Weinstein, Bruce 92n2
Wells Fargo 11, 146
Wendy Glavin Agency 23–5
Who's Who Among American High
School Students 140
Wikipedia 42, 50
Williams, Brian 80
Williams, Greer 57n10
Wilson, Chip 84, 93n15
Wohl, Jessica 93n9
WorldCom 109
WriteVest 20–21

Y-100 Pop Radio in Florida 90
YouTube 14, 83, 84